UNLEASHING THE WARRIOR WITHIN

Using the 7 Principles of Combat to
Achieve Your Goals

UNLEASHING THE
WARRIOR WITHIN

RICHARD J. MACHOWICZ

NEW YORK

Library of Congress Cataloging-in-Publication Data

Machowicz, Richard J.
    Unleashing the warrior within : using the 7 principles of combat
to achieve your goals / Richard J. Machowicz.
—1st ed.
        p.   cm.
    1. Success.   2. Combat—Miscellanea.
I. Title.
BJ1611.M245   2000
158—dc21   99-27699
                                                                CIP

ISBN 0-7868-6569-5

Book design by Ruth Lee

FIRST EDITION

10   9   8   7   6   5   4   3   2   1

For the men with green faces,
my immediate and extended family,
and Samantha, the best girl in the world.

Contents

UNLEASHING THE WARRIOR WITHIN

Introduction

The only easy day was yesterday.
—Navy SEAL Commandment

You know when hell is coming. You think about it. You watch that week get closer and closer, then the day get closer and closer. The anxiety builds, the doubt builds, the fear builds. Hell Week lasts six days and five nights, but when you're in it, it feels like the rest of your life.

Still, if you want to be a Navy SEAL, you have to go through it. I wanted more than anything to be part of the premier special operations unit in the United States military, perhaps the world. What I learned through the experience, and from the resulting ten-year SEAL career, is this: If you want something bad enough, you have the power to make it happen—no matter what other people have to say, no matter how tough the odds at first appear to be. I'm not telling you this to make you feel good, I'm not telling you this because it sounds nice. I'm telling you this because I know it's true. I've lived it. And you can, too. By using the principles in this book you'll develop the courage and confidence to unleash the warrior within you. In doing so you'll achieve more than you ever thought possible, because this is not a book about ideology. It's a philosophy of performance. It's about how to get things done.

There's an expression used by SEALs, and I knew it by heart before Hell Week even started: "The more we sweat in peace, the less we bleed in war." SEAL training may seem cruel and extreme, but it doesn't hold a candle to what actually happens in combat. SEALs have died in combat, but not one has ever been captured or left behind enemy lines. To hone us into men of that caliber, the navy was going to test our mettle and mold us through nothing short of the fires of hell. That is the reason for Hell Week, the sixth week in the six-month initial training program of Basic Underwater Demolition/SEAL Training, better known as BUD/S.

Funny, the day I walked into the navy recruiter's office I didn't know what I was asking when I thumbed through the description of naval jobs and stopped on the page that showed three tiny photos of guys holding machine guns, scuba diving, and jumping out of an airplane. "What's this?" I said. The recruiter explained that the acronym SEAL stood for sea, air, and land. "SEAL Team can attack from any environment, under any imaginable condition. The so-called 'frogmen' of World War II are the grandfathers of SEAL Team because they were the first underwater demolition units. SEAL Team was created during Vietnam to beat the Vietcong at their own game," the recruiter told me.

I was nineteen; I still had my collection of Batman comic books. I couldn't believe my ears—I could actually get paid to be a superhero? "Sign me up," I replied. "What do I have to do to get in?"

As it turns out, the odds of *anybody* getting in aren't good: Only fifteen out of every thousand navy enlistees who take the screening test to enter BUD/S pass it. And of those who do get in, more than 70 percent don't make it through. The smart money would have bet I'd be part of the 70 percent, because at six feet tall I weighed maybe 155 pounds soaking wet. In high school my performance as a student was . . . let's say uneven at best. A teacher went so far as to tell my mother I'd never amount to anything. In boot camp I quickly rose to become the recruit chief petty officer over the other enlistees, but even then I wasn't given much of a shot: During one of our required boot camp classes a big, meaty officer—the kind of guy who looks like he spends too much time in the gym—began asking everyone, "What do you want to do in the navy? What job are you going to go for?" When he looked at me, I said, "I'm going to be a Navy SEAL."

"There's no way you can be a SEAL. I know, trust me," he said with a dismissive laugh. "You're not SEAL material. You're too small, you're too skinny . . ."

"Sir, I'm going to be a SEAL, sir," I reiterated.

"There's no way. Period. I bet you a hundred thousand dollars right now there's no way you could be a SEAL."

"Sir, I'll take that bet, sir," I replied.

And if I could find him now I'd tell him to pay up, because I earned every cent of that $100,000. Never let anyone discourage you from your dreams or goals, no matter how big or small, because no one can ever guess how much you're capable of doing. You're the only one who can decide that.

Every man who's been through BUD/S shares an intimate acquaintance with "the bell." It's a huge brass bell, about a foot-and-a-half wide and two feet high. It's tied to a white detailed rope that's thick, heavy, and beautifully braided into one big knot at the bottom.

The bell has a few little scratches on it, but as a first-phase BUD/S classman, your responsibility is to make sure that bell is so clean and shiny it reflects like a mirror. Each of us had touched that bell, so we all deeply understood its importance and significance: At the end of training, each candidate rings the bell to signify he has made it, to say, "I did it." But ringing the bell before the end of training has an opposite meaning that's equally powerful: Once you ring it, the show's over. You ring that bell before the end of training, you say to the world: I quit. I can't handle it. There's no changing your mind, there's no coming back.

To remind you of this fact, all the way through the first phase of training the helmets of the candidates who have quit are lined along the compound. Your helmet is green with a white stripe down the middle and your name is stenciled on the front and back. Every time you go to clean the bell there are at least ten more helmets, ten more names to read of guys who quit even before Hell Week. In class number 136, my class, a hundred or more helmets lay stacked next to one another, forming a kind of hedge that went all the way around the compound. Every morning I'd read names of guys I knew, and it hit me that, man, if I don't stay in the game, my helmet could be there, too.

That's the image I had in my mind the day Hell started.

Coronado Island lies off the coast of San Diego. One half of it is a tourist resort, the other half is where the navy conducts the toughest training imaginable. At noon Sunday, the 120 of us from Class 136 who hadn't already dropped out found ourselves in this giant tent on the shores of Coronado.

Inside the tent, there was a persistent hiss of hushed whispers from guys trying to talk to each other; we'd all heard the legends about what happens in Hell Week. Some guys try to act cool, playing cards in the sand. Those are the guys who think they're going to waltz in and breeze right through this—it often turns out that they're the first ones to quit. On the other side are the guys who are really nervous—I was one of them. But I tried to keep my body relaxed and tell myself, Whatever it is, you've just got to do it.

Hours stretched out and most of us tried to get a couple minutes of sleep if we could. None of us had packed much in our backpacks—a pair of skivvies, maybe some socks, just some basic things to be able to hopefully change into during the week—but we used them as pillows.

Everything quieted down. People started to relax. The sun set as the day faded into early evening. It was like the lull right before the storm.

Then, *ra-ta-ta-ta! Boom! Boom!* All of a sudden machine guns were sounding off over our heads, big flash explosions went off. A violet haze hung in the air from smoke grenades. You couldn't even see your backpack, you couldn't see anybody, everybody was bumping into each other. "Get the hell out!" came this thunderous bellow. They ran us out of the tent, screaming: "Go here, go over there, you guys can't get it right, drop on the ground, get up." We were trying to do what they were telling us to do, but there was too much at once, it was impossible. They were spraying us with hoses, shooting off guns. "Hit the ocean," they ordered and we had to jump in the surf. It was a cold night, and we were freezing. After we were completely soaked, they hauled us back out and screamed at us to do push-ups, pull-ups, and sit-ups. Then, we ran back into the tent, and before our eyes they pulled out all the fresh clothes that we had packed for later in the week and had us drag them through the sand, then soak them in the dirt and salt water. After that, we were ordered to bring them all in and fold and organize them again. Then everything got kicked over and knocked all apart.

They just constantly mess with you. There was no way to do anything right. All of a sudden some guys just said "Forget this"—except they didn't say "forget"—and one or two quit right then in the first half hour. But the instructors just went on and on. We were never fast enough, always late, and that meant you were always paying for a mistake, yours or somebody else's.

I was on the brink of saying "I quit" when I first arrived for training. Then I remembered the words of Crow, the guy who helped me train to get into BUD/S. He was much older than me and he had said, "Mack, you've got to understand something. The system is designed for you to fail every single time. They're going to push you to see where your limit is." I didn't understand what he was saying at the time, but in that instant everything made sense. It's purely a survivor's game, it's about who makes it through and who doesn't. The process still irritated me, but that one little piece of advice was exactly what I needed. It let me keep a sense of perspective even when I was so tired I couldn't remember my name. Once I understood the rule, then it was just a matter of sticking to it. I told myself this: "I can only be defeated if I give up or die." And I wasn't going to give up.

During the training, we lost all concept of time and normalcy because we couldn't get a moment's break. Days turned into nights and nights turned into days. Sometimes you got sleep when you were lying down freezing, sometimes you got sleep when you were walking, believe it or not. I don't ever remember sleeping in Hell Week. I'd heard that the only way you could make it through BUD/S is to take it one evolution at a time: If you thought about what's going to happen next, you forgot to focus on where you were at the moment. And if that happened, you drowned, or you broke your leg, or you froze.

If you went anyplace, you ran. Everything was made into a drill. Not only that, but you ran together as a crew with a boat on top of your head. We lost two classmates due to broken necks—a thing that easily happens when you are running over slimy rocks and huge soft sand berms. One guy slips out, two guys slip out, and all of a sudden the entire weight of the boat comes down on one person's neck. If your team was the last to get anywhere, they threw sand in the boat, or they put in the coxswain, the boat driver, or the guy who seemed to not be carrying his share of the load, so you had to carry even more weight, ensuring that you couldn't win the next sprint. The whole thing is designed to put pressure on the boat crew so that you learn to work together as a team, and you learn that you're only as good as your weakest link. So there better not be any weak links. It was true about a team, and I understood it was also true about me, the individual. No matter how well I could do one thing, it didn't matter if my skills in other areas were weak. But above all, what mattered was this: You don't have to like it, you just have to do it. Stand up, shake it off, and keep going.

Surf torture formed the rhythm of our lives. It marked the next descent into another ring of hell, the only way we knew one drill had ended and another would begin. Everything always came back to sitting in the water, arms linked together like a barrel of monkeys to form a chain of freezing bodies. As the surf came in, it pounded you and made it hard to breathe because of all the salt water, sand, and shells that went up your nose and down your throat. When a strong wave came in, the line got snaky and uneven, but you couldn't let go. If you broke, the punishment wasn't worth it. If somebody broke you tried to grab their arm so quickly that, hopefully, the instructors wouldn't catch it. But, again, they knew the game, you didn't. They ordered you to stand up, and just when you thought you're about to go out and get warm again, they turned you around and put you back in.

One session went on for forty-five minutes, maybe an hour.

Suddenly the instructors said, "Stand up," and we marched back out of the water. "We're going to have a

race right now. First five people back don't have to go
back in the water. Anybody else, back in the ocean," the
instructors told us. I was cold and I was not going to get
back in that damn water. There was just no way. So when
they said "Go!" man, I took off like greased lightning
toward the rock jetty. Once we reached that we had to
turn around and run back to create a two-mile loop. I was
just flying, ahead of the pack, but all at once I began to
feel a burning, cutting feeling in my feet. It took me a second to realize what was happening—all the broken shells
drudged up in the surf had collected in my boots and
become tiny razor blades, slicing my heels and toes to rib-
bons. I just knew that could be a problem later—my feet
would swell and be painful. Still, anything was better than
feeling my blood turn to ice in that surf.

So I kept running, but I was losing speed. Two guys
passed me, then a third, and I said to myself, Oh crap, I'm
in real danger of not making it. Somewhere inside me
something screamed "No!" and let loose a power that felt
like a volcano erupting inside. My arms pumped. My feet
moved faster. Before I knew it I was at the line—the fourth
guy in, with another right behind me. As soon as the rest
got there they had to line back up and sit in the ocean
while the five of us were rewarded with a chance to at least
huddle and get some warmth going through our bodies
for a while.

The line between winning and losing was clear. I may
have done some damage to my feet, but it was a kind of a
morale victory that meant so much to me. It gave me a
small victory to hold on to. It provided the confidence to
know that, if I could win once, I could win again. I hud-

dled tight against the others and understood that you
have to create little moments of victory for yourself, no
matter how small or how short they last. Those are the
moments that carry you through to the next big challenge—and there's always another challenge, waiting just
around the corner.

The next hours and days blurred into one another.
You knew it was day because you were sweating and near
heat exhaustion. You knew it was night because that's
when hell freezes over.

Off the island there were metal piers that jut out into
the water, with nothing around them but ocean and sky.
The orders were to strip down to your underwear, if you
were wearing any. If you were not, too bad. Strip anyway.
Then, one by one, we were thrown into the open ocean.
"Tread water" is the only command.

After twenty minutes of that, you were hauled up on
to the metal pier and told to lie flat at attention. And so it
went, back and forth like that, about every ten minutes.
Just when you got a chance to rest for a second, you had
to do push-ups or sit-ups and then it was back in the water.
Over time it got cold, colder than you've ever been in your
life. Lying there, shaking and shivering, I looked to my left
and I looked to my right, and I only saw bodies flopping
around like fish on a deck after you've hooked them out
of the water. All of a sudden there was nothing but the
noise of *ja-ja-ja* that turned out to be the chattering of
teeth. Added to that was the sound of bodies hitting the
metal deck, making it hum like a tuning fork. One thing
was clear: This was a deliberate attempt to freeze us into
hypothermia.

• • •

Forty-eight hours later, things had only gotten harder. The instructors put us out in the ocean again, like they did on the day of the metal piers. But this time, they were not letting us out. They brought out the bell, making it as accessible as possible, within reach of any of us. "We're not going to let anybody out of here until somebody quits," the instructors yelled.

It went on for twenty minutes, then thirty minutes, and everyone was shaking and waiting for somebody to quit. Nobody would, because there was no "You can start over again," there was no coming back. You were either in the game or you were out of the game. But mind-numbing cold has a way of shattering any resolve.

"This is screwed up, forget it, forget it," guys started saying out loud up and down the line.

"Shut up, man, get it together," I yelled back. I knew all that talk would eat away at everyone's determination and make it collapse. Mine was just as much in peril as anybody else's. And, finally, the first domino fell—one guy jumped up and grabbed the rope on the bell, cracking the gong against the brass three times. *Dong, dong . . . dong.* All at once there was a stampede of who could get to that bell the fastest. A little ambulance pulled up right next to us with piping hot chocolate, coffee, and fresh donuts. The instructors offered towels and big wool blankets to warm them up, telling them they had tried hard, that anyone would understand why they'd quit. Class 136 dropped in size by eighty people within ten minutes.

Meanwhile, while it seemed our classmates were being rewarded for quitting, the few of us remaining in the water hadn't stopped shaking. We were each looking back and forth, seeing who would be the next to give it up. People had quit but they still weren't letting us out like they said they would. How long would this go on?

Somewhere in the corner of my mind came the realization that the instructors were weeding us out by playing negative games with our minds. The only way I would be able to win this one would be to play a positive game. I looked up at the moon and repeated, like a mantra, "The sun is beaming heat rays to the moon. The heat rays are bouncing off the moon like a mirror and warming my body. I'm getting a moon tan, I'm getting a moon tan, I'm a moon tan." It seemed like a pretty meager tool had for making myself warm, but it was the only one I had, and it worked. My core body temperature rose maybe one or two degrees, but it was enough for me, at 155 pounds, to stay in while hypothermia hit guys with much higher body fat percentages and they ended up quitting.

Soon the sky started turning pink like the inside of a conch shell. Dawn was breaking. I made a huge mental connection that would stay with me forever: The name of the game is to make it through the night to see the morning. It's such a big thing to create those moments of courage, because that fuels commitment. You can always do more than you think, you can always go a lot farther than you think.

It was the last day of hell, almost 122 hours had passed, and the instructors showed no signs of letting up. They brought food to us in boxed lunches and by then we'd all learned to protect our food, because if the instructors came by and you weren't paying attention, they'd kick sand at your food or spit on it with tobacco juice, leaving you to eat whatever you could stomach. All I was thinking was, Just make it a couple more hours. . . .

The lunch break went by too quickly and before we knew it we were back carrying the boats on our heads, doing this drill and that drill. By three o'clock in the afternoon the sun was starting to go down and all the instructors had to say was, "This is the worst class in the history of SEAL training! You haven't done one damn thing right! You guys are the worst maggots to ever crawl on earth!" The instructors started hammering us, leaving us in the ocean to freeze again, ordering pull-ups and push-ups when we'd get back out. By this point you were lucky if scabs and scratches didn't run up and down the length of your legs, as if somebody had spent hours just racking and racking sandpaper across your skin, making blood trickle down your legs. The lymph nodes in my legs swelled to the size of golf balls because cuts in my feet left by seashells had opened the way for infection. I doubted I would ever be able to walk again, because I couldn't move my legs. I thought, I hope this is worth it. My legs were almost frozen in one position because the swollen lymph nodes had started to cut off blood circulation to my lower body.

One instructor we called Doc Knock came up to me. He was a corpsman, the navy's version of a medic. "Do you want to quit, sailor?" he yelled.

Although every inch of my body screamed "yes," I said in the strongest voice I could manage, "No, Instructor Knock!"

"Then get up right now," Doc Knock said, picking me up with an arm around my rib cage. He gave me five minutes of his time, walking me in circles for five minutes until my legs started working again.

The sun was getting low in the sky now, and the instructors yelled, "You dirt bags still haven't got it right! You need more practice. We're going another night, and after that maybe another." Conventional wisdom said Hell Week is secured by about two o'clock in the afternoon of the last day, and it was far, far past that. Nothing had lightened up, it was only getting harder. Everyone was probably thinking exactly what I was: This is unbelievable. They put us back in for more surf torture and we looked at one another, trying to quell this rising sense of panic that, "Man, this could actually go into another night . . ."

Then all of a sudden we heard a roar behind us. Over the megaphone came the order, "Turn around!" We turned to see a figure rising over the sand hill. It was the captain of the naval amphibious base. I knew then I had made it. Tears just started flowing out of my eyes. I had done something no one, not even I, knew I could do. Again I heard the voices telling me I was too small, that there was no way I could stick it out. Then the voices faded; from that moment on there was no doubt I could measure up. No one would ever be able to take that from me, ever.

The end of Hell Week was the beginning of my ten-year career as a SEAL. When I left the navy, I served for a time as a personal protection specialist for a number of business leaders and celebrities. Drawing from my experience as a SEAL hand-to-hand combat instructor and from almost two decades perfecting various forms of martial arts (including arnis, muay thai, and jujitsu), I have also created a self-protection training system called Bukido™.

The word "Bukido" was formed out of Japanese characters to describe the journey an individual must take to bring out the "warrior within." I designed Bukido as a serious combat training system to be used for self-protection and in deadly situations, not for sport or tournament amusement. All of my Bukido clients are extremely successful in their fields of expertise, whether they are scientists, entrepreneurs, lawyers, psychologists, or journalists. Despite—or maybe because of—their own accomplishments, each has been intrigued by my background: How, they want to know, did I manage to motivate myself to such a high performance standard year after year? What is it like, they ask me, to commit every fiber, every molecule of being, to completing a goal? How do you train yourself to not ever consider the option of quitting under the most stressful situations?

I believe the reasons people make it through BUD/S are so personal they never share them with their teammates. I certainly didn't go around asking, and nobody asked me why I made it. They only cared that you made it. We never really sat around analyzing why we made it: "I tell ya, HoJo, the reason I made it through is because I had a miserable childhood" wasn't exactly conversation over a couple beers. But for someone to drive themselves to those extremes, I believe they're ultimately trying to create something of absolute value. They're trying to define a life for themselves, to establish a different, higher standard for the rest of their lives. Being a warrior is not about the act of fighting. *It's about being so prepared to face a challenge and believing so strongly in the cause you are fighting for that you refuse to quit.*

When I look at why I made it through Hell Week, why I went the distance through the pain threshold, through the cold threshold, why I pushed myself and continued to keep going, it was because it was something I really wanted. I didn't have the words to describe it at that point, but when I look back now I see that I was clearly driven by the image of me someday wearing a big gold trident on my chest. I loved the thought of the respect I would earn from others having accomplished this. I loved the fact that, unlike money or fame or material possessions, this accomplishment could never, ever be diminished or taken away from me. This experience was not something that I was forced to survive; I could have gotten out of it anytime. I put myself in the situation. The value wasn't just about surviving, it was about choice. It was about the fact that I tested myself and I passed the test. I would always be a SEAL, I'm a SEAL now, even though I'm not doing the job. That means not being the strongest, or the fastest, or even the smartest. It's simply a matter of being the one who does not quit—and that's an ability available to anyone.

Where did I get the mental ability to make it through the toughest situations? SEAL training doesn't bestow this quality; they want to see who already possesses it. That surprised me when I realized it. I went into the military looking for masters, the people who would deliver all the secrets of the universe. It came from studying the martial arts for more than half my life—you're always told there is a guru out there who will teach you if you do x, y, and z. As a kid I would go from dojo to dojo. I would do x, y, and z and would learn some really valuable things, and learn a lot of things that weren't really valuable at all. I came to realize there are a lot of people out there with a lot of great information. They are called teachers. In SEAL Team, I was trained by some of the greatest teachers on the planet and had available to me the finest resources that money can buy. But, ultimately, to find a master you have to find that master within yourself. Find what works best for you. Always remember that you are trying to master yourself, not find a master for you.

The concepts that you will read about in this book are tools I developed to master myself. They have been tested in combat under the worst situations imaginable. Most have been written in blood. Along the way I've discovered that people who have created success never tell you you can or can't do it. They only want to know how badly you want it. It's the people who are afraid to take the chance or have inherited someone else's success who tell you about everything you've got to lose. The people who are afraid of risking it all quit the first time the going gets rough. It's not until you risk it all and go for the thing you really want that life becomes unlimited. All the shackles are released.

Other books on the market have given eyewitness accounts of SEAL Teams in combat, as well as autobiographical works on SEAL careers. *Unleashing the Warrior Within* offers something no other book has: A plan for thinking like a SEAL—at least, one SEAL—so that you, too, can reach incredible goals, to "live on a different, higher standard," and achieve more of what you want out of life. Bukido students learn these ideas in the process of mastering a physical discipline. While it's impossible to bring the full visceral impact of my teachings to the page,

I guarantee that if you participate completely in the drills incorporated in the book and apply them daily, something inside you will change. By the time you finish the chapters that follow, you will have gone through a seven-step process to free that warrior within yourself.

Everybody knows life isn't easy. Sometimes it even feels like a war. Often we have to fight to make even our simplest goals and dreams possible. But if you know how to fight, and know what you're fighting for, you can always come out on top. I'm going to teach you how to fight for what you love.

Chapter 1

The Three Dynamic Elements of Combat

> . . . if one advances confidently in the directions of his dreams, and endeavors to live the life which he has imagined, he will meet with a success unexpected in common hours.
>
> —*Henry David Thoreau*

From nuclear warfare to hand-to-hand combat, there is only one guiding strategy: targets, weapons, movement. If you know what your target is, that will dictate which weapon you use. Once you have your weapon, the weapon will dictate how you move it.

This was the underlying principle behind everything I learned becoming a SEAL—in scout/sniper operations, in the Naval Special Warfare Combat Fighting Instructor Course, in land, mountain, desert, and arctic warfare, and in counterterrorist operations. Understanding these concepts—targets dictate weapons, weapons dictate movement—saved my life during everything from a screwed-up skydive to a couple of nasty bar fights in Southeast Asia. But never was this important idea clearly and simply stated.

Targets dictate weapons, weapons dictate movement is the fundamental principle behind succeeding in anything. But I didn't read this in a book or hear it articulated from any admiral. The person who led me to form the Three Dynamic Elements of Combat™, the basis for all Bukido, was a forty-five-year-old suburban executive assistant named Donna.

What ultimately became Bukido started off as a little business in which I took on beginners and gave them great self-protection skills very quickly. I had a shoestring budget and started teaching out of my garage. Most of the people who signed up were men and a few were bodyguards who wanted more know-how. I was teaching students the way I had been taught, but it was too severe for civilians, too demanding. The students were picking up skills, but it was going very, very slowly.

My mother set up a seminar on rape prevention with me for a group of her coworkers. The women were like my mom—they didn't want any fancy stuff, they just wanted to know how to prevent or survive a rape or attack. The tools I had available to teach them were traditional martial arts and my diverse SEAL training, and none of those would create skills instantaneously. They all required a certain level of athletic ability most people just don't spend time developing. I refined a program that was very basic, but even though the students were very responsive and complimentary and I regularly had twenty-five to fifty people sign up, I never had the feeling they knew enough. If a situation truly got ugly, most would be shut down by fear and forget the basic strikes that could offer them any protection from an attacker.

One student, Donna, was very committed and wanted to develop better physical skills, so she signed up for private training. I began by teaching her a set series of movements—basic boxing punches, grappling and martial arts kicks, repeating and repeating the drill in order to perfect her movement. She got to the point where she moved wonderfully, a regular Rocky. Yet, when I grabbed her, everything went out the window. She panicked like a deer in headlights. So I worked with her on more movement, better weapons—more knee strikes, a lightning jab—but when things got rough, the results were the same. We were both frustrated.

"I'm just not getting this. I can't do it," she said one day in disgust.

I turned away from her for an instant to cool off, because I wanted to yell, "Of course you can! Just do it!" But instead, I did something else.

I whirled back around and grabbed her by the throat. And when I grab, I don't play. I don't feign. This may seem mean or macho or intense, but what I learned as a SEAL is to train as close to reality as possible because that is the only way to condition yourself to perform during a real situation. You might get cuts and bruises in the process, but it will someday save your hide.

Her face turned red, she flailed against my grip.

"Take my eyes out," I growled. "Do something, anything!"

Then, wham. Like a laser, without any indecision, she took the most direct and immediate route: Her hand jutted out to bury her fingers in my eyes. Instantly my hands dropped away from her throat.

It was pure, mainline result. She had stopped thinking about where her hand was supposed to be, or how she was supposed to stand, or where she was supposed to move next.

She just got results.

It was phenomenal. I started doing this to all my students before I taught them any other skill, and without fail they all did the same thing—they managed to get a finger into my eye and make me release them. Sometimes they were slow, sometimes they were awkward, sometimes they looked funny, but they did it. Each got the result.

The lesson was obvious: Get everything out of the way of the target. Then you will clearly see what weapons you need and what movement is required. But doubt and second-guessing where you're supposed to be, or how you're supposed to be doing something, obscures what you need to go for. Everything becomes difficult and overwhelming when you don't really understand your target or haven't defined your intention. The more complicated something is, the more difficult it is to bring into reality.

Bukido was born from this realization. Without a focused mind, results are happenstance, unreliable. Thought precedes every action, so in order to focus the mind, you need a way to streamline your thinking. Bukido is about prioritizing the process so you do things in an effective order to get results more efficiently—which means getting results faster.

This strategy also guides personal achievement: First you decide on a goal. After that, you look at what tools you need to achieve it, then you put those weapons in motion. After doing an introduction drill on the Three

Dynamic Elements of Combat, one of my clients said she realized in retrospect that she had already done this in order to go after her biggest dream: To see her byline in the *New Yorker* magazine. She was conscious of the fact that she picked her target, but she had been unconscious of everything she did to make that a reality. When she finally saw her name in print, it seemed to her to only be good luck, forgetting she had honed her weapon—her skills—and she had positioned herself to be in the right place at the right time to show off those skills. She forgot the years she spent in school to become a better writer, that she wrote articles in other publications, met others in her field, and over years developed a network. That target, the image of her name in the magazine, wasn't something she necessarily thought about every day, but it was in the back of her mind, guiding her movement in the direction of that target.

Once she picked her target, she mobilized the skills she would need to knock down that target. When we make the conscious choice to pick the target, to sharpen our weapon, to make our movement efficient we get results faster than relying on an unconscious process. Those results are much slower and appear more happenstance. We do this every day and aren't even aware of it. Here's a rudimentary example: Please go turn on your bathroom light.

Was it difficult to hit the target?
Did I tell you which hand to use?
Did I tell you how to move your arm?
Did I tell you how to get to the bathroom?
Did I tell you to walk, run, jump?

The answers to all are, obviously, no. Did you turn
the light on anyway? Of course. The directive simply told
you what to focus on and a million tiny actions occurred,
resulting in something being accomplished. Why? Because
it was target-driven. The more I habitually condition
myself for the tasks in the future, the better my skills are.
The better my skills are, the easier the task is to perform
and the less energy it takes to perform it. Think of when
you were a child; turning on a light switch was as difficult
as anything you could imagine. But once you could do it,
it required no energy. The habitual action made the coordination of movement so easy and fluid it required no
effort or thought.

If I told you what you had to do and made you perform it to an exact specification, the task would become
more difficult simply because now it would be more complicated. Life is often chaotic and unpredictable. But once
you pick a target, that target will lead you to the next steps
if you let it. I teach each of my students that I don't care
what they have to do to hit the target, just hit the target
and knock it down. If you ask ten Academy Award-winning
actors how they got to the moment where the Oscar was
handed to them, you'll hear ten different stories. Likewise,
if you ask ten millionaires how they became rich, they'll all
have different tales to tell. You can't afford to abandon a
target in the process of knocking it down, because when
you do that you lose the power of focus and concentration.
What happens if you keep shifting from target to target?
Think about the domino effect: When you shift targets,
what does that automatically do to your weapons? What
does that automatically do to your movement? It throws

everything into chaos. If you're shifting from one target to another target, there's no way to successfully deploy your weapons and movement with purpose. The ability to focus is lost. Diffuse a laser and it is just light.

On the other hand, movement—that is, how you get your weapons to your target—is ultimately flexible. The only thing to keep in mind is balance, so you don't risk everything, you don't fall on your face. You stay flexible. When you are flexible you'll find the way to knock down your targets. While role models can be a guide whose experience you can learn from, understand that you are on your own path. Think flexible.

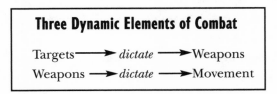

Three Dynamic Elements of Combat

Targets ⟶ *dictate* ⟶ Weapons
Weapons ⟶ *dictate* ⟶ Movement

Imagine a punch thrown from a boxer like Mike Tyson, or a kick of Bruce Lee's. Lethal, right? Wrong. No matter how powerful they are, they don't have any effect—*unless they hit the target*. The difference between success and failure comes down to just one thing: Your ability to focus on a target. The more laserlike the focus, the quicker the target is attained. The reason is simple: You don't diffuse your energy if you precisely define what it is you're going after. Here is a systematic way to evaluate whether a target is one you really want to go for or not, taken from the way a SEAL commander evaluates whether or not a target is attainable. The process is the same whether the target is obliterating an enemy's weapon stockpile, landing a business account, or even getting a date for the company picnic.

Navy SEALs who undergo an exclusive course called Special Operations Target Analysis Studies are taught to assess targets through a no-fail matrix known by the acronym CARVER: Criticality, Accessibility, Recognizability, Vulnerability, Effect on the Overall Mission, and Return on Effort or Recuperability. *This is the way you figure out what target counts the most.* Here's how these elements factor into assessing the value of any military target, large or small:

> **Criticality:** How vital is this to the overall mission? If I hit this target, is it going to contribute to achieving ultimate victory?
>
> **Accessibility:** How easily can I get to this target? How easy is it for me to hit this target?
>
> **Recognizability:** How easy is it for me to find this target? How easy or difficult is it for me to recognize the things I need to do in order to knock this target down?
>
> **Vulnerability:** What is the degree of force needed to destroy the target? Can it be easily finished within a certain time frame? What is the extent of the resources needed to knock this target down?
>
> **Effect on the Overall Mission:** To what degree will the destruction of this target affect my enemy? How much closer will this get us to ending the war?
>
> **Return on Effort (what SEALs call recuperability):** Can the enemy recover from the destruction of this target? If so, how long will it take? What is the return on the initial investment of resources, and when will I see it?

These are the principles I use to teach students the primary targets in Bukido. Different areas on the body were evaluated using CARVER in order to define the best targets—those that will be consistently available and produce an instant result. The primary targets are what we refer to in the singular simply as Eyes-Throat-Groin. Each one of them is critical for the body to function; accessible with arms and legs, which are the four major weapons we all carry around; recognizable on anyone; and each of them is extremely vulnerable to attack. Each, when destroyed, has a devastating overall effect on the body. And guess what? Every one of them, when severely damaged, will require some time for an attacker to recover. All three targets become part of one thought, so that eventually students don't even have to hear Eyes-Throat-Groin, they just look to see which of those three targets are open, then they go. If one is closed, it's likely two are open. But if two are closed, one is always going to be open. By hitting these targets we're going to have a major effect on the system that will then open up other targets.

We prioritize our targets to make things very easy, so that we never forget where we are or where we're going next. In Bukido we concentrate on really destroying at least one of our first-strike targets before we proceed to anything else. Remember, when you're battling for your life there are no referees or judges. It is not about performing for the fans. It's about getting home alive.

You might be thinking, That's great if I get attacked, but what does this have to do with me getting what I want out of life? In fact, that's what a student of mine, who is an actor, asked me one day after class. "This is all great if my boss is Charlie Manson. But Richard, how does this help me figure out what I want?" he joked, but his tone told me that underneath the smiling exterior was a man who really wanted answers.

So we sat down with a pen and a piece of paper, and I said, "Give me five things you're struggling with right now."

A lot of things were weighing on him—he felt he needed to get in better shape, there was a beachfront property he was considering buying, his agent was driving him crazy so he was thinking about getting another one, and, almost as an afterthought, he mentioned that he'd like to convince a certain producer to use him for a new project.

"Let's call these 'targets,' " I told him. "What we're going to do is analyze these targets and prioritize them using CARVER, so you know which one is the most important for you to take care of right away."

I asked him a series of questions. We gave a value to every answer based on 1 to 5; 5 being the most valuable and/or easiest to attain, and 1 being the least valuable and/or the most difficult to attain. I offered just a few words of guidance: "Remember, for this to work, you have to be *ruthlessly* honest with yourself."

I began with the issue of getting in shape. Criticality was the first factor to assess. "What I want you to think about is how critical is the accomplishment of this target? Will hitting this target improve your life in a significant way?"

"On a scale of one to five? Maybe a two," he said.

Then I moved on to accessibility. "How accessible are the tools or the facility you have to get it? Do you have ultimate control over this or does it require other people to be involved? Who really does the work it will take to get this done? True power is recognizing who or what really wields the authority to make things happen."

"This one's all about me," he replied.

"So it's very accessible?"

"Yeah. Let's give it a five."

The next question was one of recognizability. "Will you recognize when you are doing things that help you get closer to being in shape? Is what you have to do clearly defined?"

"Tape my mouth shut?" he laughed. "Being honest? I know what I have to do. Everybody knows that. We've all read the magazines. It's a five."

"Okay. So how vulnerable is this target? How much can get in the way of you accomplishing this target? Or, does going after this target make you vulnerable in any way?"

"It's a two. Lots of things can get in the way, like when I'm crunched for time or really stressed," he said.

Then we needed to determine how getting in shape would, ideally, affect his overall happiness and well-being. "How close does this take you to where you need to go?"

"It would lower my cholesterol no doubt, and I wouldn't feel so sluggish, so I'll give it a three."

Then I asked him about return on effort—how much time, money, and/or effort will it take before I see a result? Will I overextend myself going for this target? How easy and how soon will it be for me to see a return on my effort? Will the rewards I get from taking out this target be worth the investment of time and energy I use to reach it?

Here he had to pause. "If I looked at myself in the mirror, it might take just a couple months to see a result—

if I hire a trainer. Without one, it might take a while longer, but I could do it. I'll give it a four."

We went through his remaining targets the same way, ending up with this chart:

Carver Matrix

Targets	Critical	Access	Recognize	Vulnerable	Effect Happiness	Return	Total
Get in Shape	2	5	5	2	3	4	21
Beach Property	2	3	5	2	2	2	16
Better Agent	3	2	2	1	4	2	14
Convince Producer	4	3	3	2	5	5	22

The chart revealed some pretty interesting things. The target he initially considered almost an afterthought, a kind of pie-in-the-sky wish, turned out to be the most critical target weighing on him at the moment. The items with the two highest scores, getting in shape and having the producer consider him, showed not only what was most critical but what was also relatively easy to knock down. Finding a better agent and buying a beachfront property, once he sat down and thought about it, weren't ultimately that important at the moment. He could stop worrying about them and focus on what he really wanted and could attain.

Pick four targets that you are interested in, get a piece of paper, and ruthlessly fill out a CARVER matrix of your own. It's very important to go through and answer all of the questions on page 26 in order to get the most complete, objective view possible. What you initially thought was the easiest or most important issue might turn out to be not as big a deal once you've completed the CARVER matrix. Or, it may turn out to be more difficult than it's worth. Things may change, of course, but you can't worry about that. You've got to deal with the reality at that moment to plan for the future.

The answers will also reveal where the strategic weaknesses in any given target might hide. Once you get the broad view of the target and can see every aspect in context, you know what you're really dealing with. And when you know what you're dealing with, you can always compensate and adjust your plan.

In my experience, what is most critical and what I think will have the greatest impact on my overall happiness are the two most telling factors. They tell me how much I really want this target. Desire is the fuel that drives me to find the solution to the other factors. If this target is truly critical and truly affects happiness, then I will find ways to make it accessible—in other words, I will make it happen, and I will also make sure I don't overextend myself in the process.

If two targets are both critical and hitting them would have a high effect on your happiness, go with the easier— that is, more accessible—one first. You can build on that success—nothing breeds confidence like accomplishment.

The reason I teach that we must ruthlessly evaluate the target is to properly assess its value. Very often I see people make a target of goals with little value. Here's what I mean: getting home from work to watch "must-see" TV. Yes, it can be entertaining, but ultimately, what does this do for your sense of achievement in life? I guarantee that if you make that target critical, you'll be in front of the tube on Tuesday night without fail. The sad thing about making a target like this critical is that it is easy to attain. Like the old saying, we tend to go down the path of least resistance. You'll be an extremely successful TV viewer. If that brings fulfillment, who am I to stop you? But if you can focus your energy on getting in front of the TV, imagine what could happen if you focused that same energy, one night a week, to achieving something you really want. At least you would be in the process of moving toward something of value. Inch by inch, piece by piece.

Cynicism, that "it's-not-important" attitude, is like a cancer because it eats away at your sense that achieving something counts. When that happens, failure can't be far behind. For example, why does a goal like weight loss have such a high failure rate? Because people don't consider losing weight critical to the function of their lives. It would be nice, sure, but critical? It's only when it becomes critical— your doctor orders you to lose thirty pounds because you've developed diabetes or you can't fit into your wedding dress and the ceremony is only three weeks away—that people act and succeed. If you look closely at any of those "before-and-after" stories so popular in magazines about people who have lost weight and kept it off, you'll notice that each story always has a turning point, a moment where the issue became absolutely central to the way that person functions in the world. Some factor in their lives forced this act to become critical and the central focus in their lives.

There was an absolute value placed on their given target and they allowed nothing to get in the way. It almost seemed—and in some cases actually was—a matter of life and death. The accomplishment of the goal was made black or white, there was nothing relative about it. Hitting that target became nonnegotiable—it *had* to happen.

So often we wait for an expert to give us permission to act upon something that is critical to our lives. Weight loss is a perfect example: We go to a doctor. The doctor prescribes losing ten pounds as a preventative step to ward off cardiovascular disease or high blood pressure. All of a sudden it's like we're given the go-ahead to start looking after our health.

Stop looking to others to give you permission to go after the target you want to knock down. You are your own master. Set the target up, then knock it down. It really is that simple once you stop waiting for permission. Stop waiting for the perfect moment. Stop waiting until you can move perfectly. Stop saying you'd do it if only you had a sharper weapon. Stop waiting for the ideal situation. There is no such thing.

Let me mention a quick word about weapons and movement: Develop your weapons to take out specific targets. One simple concept to think about is that in war, weapons are chosen based on the fact that they can hurt the enemy and not hurt you. When developing your skills and using them, make sure they can take out the target without you getting hurt in the process. For instance, if you rely on skills like manipulating and lying to people to get what you want, guess what? It's only a matter of time before that explodes in your face. Developing skills like attention to detail, strategic thinking, and effective communication creates powerful weapons that, when aimed at a specific target, yield dramatic results that you can be proud of. As for movement, it should be effective first, efficient second. Time and practice make movement efficient.

Once you have decided that a particular target is absolutely critical to your life and happiness, you must make it your mission to achieve it. This mission must become the central focus of your time and energy. Once declared and pursued, this mission will unveil the several smaller targets that you need to knock down along the way in order to accomplish your mission. After you have declared what your mission is, there is only one thing you absolutely need to understand in order to jump-start your mission. When I went through BUD/S, we were told there was only one secret to making it through the training. It wasn't anything we could put in a backpack, or study up on. It was guts. *All you need is guts.*

But what does that mean? I discovered what that meant every moment of my ten-year SEAL career. It was just a feeling at first, an intensity of being. I had to find a way to articulate that to my students. If you can answer yes to each of these three questions, you have the guts you need to take out your target:

Gut Check

✓ Are you willing to make a *choice*?
✓ Do you have the *courage* to start?
✓ Can you make the *commitment* to finish?

A lot of people make a choice. Few people have the courage to start. Rarely do people have the commitment to finish. The people who do are those who have the guts to get through the losses along the way in order to reach the victory at the end. Now that you understand that targets dictate which weapons you choose, and the type of weapons you have dictate how they must be used, you have to appreciate one more thing: It's not until you make a target a matter of life and death that you end up living.

Chapter 2

Crush the Enemy Called Fear

I must not fear. Fear is the mind-killer. Fear is the little-death that brings total obliteration. I will face my fear. I will permit it to pass over me and through me. And when it has gone past, I will turn the inner eye to see its path. Where the fear has gone, there will be nothing. Only I will remain.

—*Frank Herbert,* Dune

This was my seventeenth jump. I've done hundreds of others since, but this is the one I'll never forget.

We were in freefall training, called HALO for *H*igh *A*ltitude, *L*ow *O*pen. HALO is one of many different methods the military uses as a way of inserting special operations troops into hostile territory. The reason HALO is important is that it's a very sneaky way to get to a target. When an airplane flies low you can easily see the paratroopers jumping out, but when the plane flies high, and the jumpers wait until they're only 1,500 feet above the ground to open their chutes, something very different happens. Flying at up to 30,000 feet, if you see anything at all from the ground you might just glimpse an airplane going by. What you won't see are the heavily armed troops spilling out in a string across the sky.

After two weeks of ground school, where we learned what malfunctions we could potentially face and how to deal with them, our job was to practice. I call it a "job" but at that point in the process they were basically fun jumps. We didn't have tons of equipment on as we learned to get comfortable flying through the air without wings.

Everything had been going great so far. I was having a blast. I thought, This is a lot of fun, I'm loving the tremendous adrenaline rush I get through my body each and every time I jump. The instructor, Rico, would always tell us, "Today the devil holds all the cards, to beat him you've got to cheat him." When I was on the ground all I could think was, How soon can I cheat that bastard again?

That day we were working on formations, coming together in groups of three or four in the air, then separating. I'm thinking about my routine. Two other guys and I are supposed to come out together as a three-man team and create a triangle. Then we're going to fly away, rotate, and catch each other a different way before flying off in "delta," which is when you put your hand at your sides and become a human bullet.

I hear the drone of the jet engines of the C141 and look around. Some guys have their eyes closed, some guys are talking, some guys are working on their formations, some guys are nervously fiddling with their straps. We were issued old PC Mark 2s for training—they tie very tight to the body with nylon straps and metal rigging hooks that dig in everywhere. You cinch the rig down into your body because you want to keep it nice and close. If it's loose, when the chute opens it will feel as though someone is literally trying to unzip your body. The straps come over your shoulders, across your chest, and then you have a reserve parachute across your belly.

Like most everybody else I just rested my hands on the reserve and tried to look like I was taking a nap. One of the reasons you sort of close your eyes is, of course, to look like you're really cool, but you're also genuinely trying to relax your body. The fact of the matter is, you're jumping out of an airplane, you could die. It's hard to completely get out of your mind that eventually you're going to be stepping from an airplane at 15,000 feet, and if you don't do everything right you don't get a second chance.

Some guys are being boisterous, pumping up for that moment when we get right up to the ramp and we're about to leave behind a perfectly good airplane. I was no exception. On my black helmet I've got a piece of tape that has Japanese writing on the side and a big red kamikaze character in the center.

Behind the wall of machismo, thoughts creep in and out. You have to get along very well with your parachute, and you want your parachute to get along very well with you. If that parachute doesn't get along, you at least want the reserve to get along with you *really* well, because that's the final one to save you. I see somebody rehearsing his drills and it occurs to me, You know, that's a pretty good idea. I start rehearsing, too, and so does everybody else. The sudden desire to rehearse is like a disease, it's catching.

Just then you can hear the bolts unlocking on the hydraulic door for the ramp. The top part of the ramp goes up and the bottom part goes down, unfolding to create a flat little place with quite a view. The toxic, diesel smell of the burning JP5 fuel assaults your nose. You can hear the rushing of the air. It's weird. All of a sudden you can't hear anything, but you think you can hear everything. When you stand up you can't actually hear your boots landing on the metal floor, but you know the *clink-clink* is supposed to be there as you walk. Your ears strain to hear it.

Everybody starts to line up. We again rehearse our little routine and go over malfunction drills. You're trying to keep your mind busy so you're not just sitting, waiting. As you wait, the fear grows. But if you have tasks that keep your mind focused on your objective, the fear withers.

The jump master looks back and yells, "Two minutes!" There is no way you can hear him so he holds up two fingers. He returns to sticking his head out the ramp. The first time I saw a jump master I thought, Man, that has to be the scariest job on earth. Is he thinking about being blown away? Since then I've discovered that the more you're in charge, the more things you're focused on getting done and the less you're focused on all the things that could go wrong.

With the countdown on, everybody in line begins the gear check. You turn the guy in front of you around and check to make sure his pins line up properly, no pins bent up. And you go down the line, checking one another. This is standard no matter what you're doing—we're always taking care of one another, because these are the "teams." It's important to have somebody watching your back.

The jump master throws out a streamer to check the wind. "One minute," he yells, and now you take a deep breath in. Everybody takes a hit off of an oxygen bottle as it passes. This helps your brain to think clearly, because the air is thin at 15,000 feet.

Before you know it the jump master yells, "Thirty seconds," and we group up, grabbing onto one another's shoulders. Clouds race by, but the ground goes slowly. The buildings and cars below look like the miniatures you played with as a kid. Just for a split second you remember that concrete is hard.

The jump master gives the nod and yells "Go!" There's a sucking in of breath, then you step out and *whooom*. Reflex wants you to close your eyes and wait until it is all over before you open them again, but you fight it and win. The first moment out of the plane is like being in a washing machine. You get a sensation of being yanked and dragged around. Finally you relax, you reach terminal velocity, and the wind current cradles you.

Suddenly you become conscious of your body. You look at your buddy's face and it's going *blu-blu-blu*, shock waves of air hitting skin at 130 miles an hour. We perform our rehearsed routine then clear away from one another.

I look down at my altimeter, 2,500 feet, no problem. Waving off, I look up; nobody is ahead of me, no one is to the side of me, and, most importantly, no one is above me. I reach down, find the main parachute's ripcord, and pull my chute.

Nothing happens.

I say to myself, You're supposed to pull it no more than three times. I lock on to the ripcord once more. I pull.

It doesn't release. *Oh, man.*

I say, Okay, this third time I'm going to make this thing release. At this point I retract the hand I was using to keep myself stable in the air so I can use both hands to pull. But what's happening to my head? It's going straight down to earth. I'm picking up speed dramatically. Where is my parachute? On my back. Where are my feet? Directly in line with the parachute when it opens.

Bad mistake. A beginner's mistake. A dead man's mistake.

Wham! And I jerk the parachute free. Suddenly I can feel it—my chute wraps around my foot. And I'm just thinking, Oh God. This is a bad parachute malfunction for one reason: I can't pull a reserve parachute, because if I pull my reserve parachute, I know what happens. It goes up in line with the first one. If my reserve gets tied up in my main parachute, I'm steak tartare. There's no doubt about it. It's crystal clear.

Before I can cut away the first parachute, I have to clear it off my body. I can feel it flapping around on my legs, on my back, doing everything but opening.

That's when it attacked me: The Panic. Decision making, rational thinking, start to shut down. I've got one thing going for me: I have been trained by the best in the world. The better your conditioning, the better your training, the quicker you get through that moment when panic seizes you. But that split second it takes to recognize fear and move past it feels like eternity.

Then, the rush kicks in. "Okay," I quickly say to myself. What do I have to do? The answer: Get this parachute off. How do I do it? I slowly reach down with my right hand toward my leg so I can get the parachute off from where it's wrapped around my foot and my shin. I have to be careful because if I flip over into the parachute then I'm wearing the whole thing, completely tied up, going headfirst straight to the ground. I've got to be meticulous and focused. Everything in my world is focused on clearing my leg and staying in balance. Just for a second I see the ground, but tear my eyes away. I know ground rush, that hypnotic pull of gravity, just sucks you right in.

Finally it comes free. The parachute deploys and all of a sudden I feel it clear. Now I'm traveling anywhere from 150 to 180 miles an hour, with the chute deployed. The next two seconds seem to take minutes. Even though the parachute is released and it's slowing me down, I'm still headed to earth head first. My body is going in one direction, the parachute is going in the other direction, and then—

Whip! It finally catches and hurls me upright. The only thing I can do is just go limp. If I had kept my body tense I would have gone right back through the risers of the chute and been caught like a dolphin in a tuna net. I look down at my altimeter. Five hundred feet left, time to guide my parachute and land on the ground.

Dirt never felt so good.

It's a given that fear exists for every one of us. But never for a moment think that if you're afraid of something, that fear is somehow a warning and will save you. Good evaluation of past experiences makes for good decisions, period. And it's good decisions that will save you.

Why do we think it will hurt when we fall out of an airplane and hit the ground? We remember how much it hurt when we fell out of a chair, or fell off our bikes when we were kids. Thus, we perceive that dropping out of a plane is obviously going to multiply that pain by a factor of about, oh, let's say a million.

If during freefall training I had been truly afraid of jumping out of an airplane, if I was truly convinced that the likelihood of dying was greater than the likelihood of living, would I have jumped in the first place? No. You don't have to jump out of an airplane to conquer that fear of death and embrace the experience of life. But you do have to live and act in spite of fear, whatever that fear may be. When I'm afraid to ask a girl out, I feel stupid because I didn't ask her out. If I back down from a bully because I'm afraid, that fear and frustration stays with me for hours and hours, because it was a failure to act. Fear is not a true indicator of danger, evaluated experience is. If you let your world become constricted by fear, fear has already won. You're trapped in a kind of living death.

Fear is by definition defensive and reactive. During my bad jump, the thought that kept repeating was, What do I have to get done? What do I have to get done? What do I have to get done. . . . The more you think about fear, the more you start to shut down your thinking. We know that a thought precedes every action, so if I'm spending thoughts on fear I'm reducing the availability of thoughts needed to take effective action. As a result, the less ability you're going to bring to solving the situation presented to you.

There's a well-known saying among men who have been in the military: In combat, a man's brains turn to water and run out his ears. Warriors train at such an intense level exactly for this reason—if you don't know how to handle it, fear will shut you down.

One of my clients came to me exactly for this reason. A reclusive inventor by nature, Julio* was in his element in the early days of his own small audio business, when it was just about coming up with an idea, trying it out in his shop, and fine-tuning the details. But Julio started to feel uneasy when it blossomed into a real enterprise with the pressures of employing other people and having to meet complete strangers to whom he had to sell his ideas.

Thinking he was analyzing his business by imagining all the things that could go wrong and why someone would not buy his product, Julio would spend hours and hours imagining situations that might happen. Soon he felt extremely nervous every time he had to talk to a prospective client. Slow sales in the beginning led him to imagine he would have to let his two employees go, and that his family would lose the investment of capital they'd put behind him. This led to anxiety so strong he would wake up at night with chest pain. Beginning with the seeds of unease, Julio's fear grew like a weed until it strangled off his decision-making ability. He literally became afraid to pick up the phone. What he needed was to find a way to break down his fear, understand the nature of it, and then move through it to his target of developing a successful business.

Fear is the perception of an unknown threshold. The more unknowns, the greater the fear. The unknown why, when, what, where, who, and how much have more to do with fear than the actual task or danger itself. The less

---

*Some names and other identifying details have been changed in the interest of privacy.

control we have the greater our perceived fear. This is why surprise quickly gives way to fear.

Suppose you're growing up in an unstable environment, like an alcoholic home, where actions are completely unpredictable. As you get older you recognize there are indicators for behavior, but when you're very young you can't guess what that alcoholic is going to do. Again, everything is outside of your sphere of reference. You don't know how bad it's going to hurt, when it's going to come, what is going to take place. It almost always catches you by surprise, and fear takes root in surprise. The more fear you have in your thoughts, the more fear is transmitted to your mind or body, so the less you're able to think. The more diminished your thinking, the more diminished your action. Fear causes us to recoil, to move away from. If you're thinking "move backward" in your head, you're moving backward in your body.

Surprise is a major component of fear. Warriors know this and use it to their advantage. In SEAL Team we are taught there are Three Elements of a Successful Attack: **Surprise, Speed,** and **Violence of Action**. If you want to cause chaos or if somebody is trying to cause chaos to you, these three factors will do it. The reasons are simple once you think about it: The greater your surprise, the greater your biochemical stress is going to be. The greater your biochemical stress, the greater your fear. It's just that simple.

Speed is the next factor. If something comes at you very quickly there is going to be a moment where you freeze. Speed allows very little time for you to properly evaluate what is happening and act on it.

The final factor is violence of action. It has to do with the intensity and full commitment of going after a target.

It is extreme in nature. The objective is to leave no possibility for recovery.

Surprises do happen in life, but that is not the same as saying life is full of surprises. If you live it that way, if you live life without planning the most basic actions, you live life purely as a reaction. If you say to yourself, I'm just going to react to whatever happens, then you're going to face a lot more fear.

You don't choose to live through a firefight, where bullets rain down like deadly hail, by luck. You ensure your survival by taking charge of moments. We all know that you can't control everything in life, but just as it's true that we can tolerate a lot more pain than imaginable when it's necessary, it's also true that you control a lot more than you think. I see students all the time who live in a world where they only want to take charge of maybe 20 percent of life. "I have to go to work in the morning." Presto! You wake up and go to work in the morning. It's amazing that people take charge of things all the time, but they're not aware of it. Yet, they are not willing to take control of the biggest things they want in life. It's easier to say you can't control those things than to say, "I have to control them, so I have to take the responsibility to get things done." I can't control other people and I can't control a situation. But I can control my actions in that situation. Often I've found that's enough.

I developed a simple formula to teach my students like Julio they have the ability to improve the outcome of every situation that they face. The **Improved Outcome Formula** essentially works like this: There are three elements that come together to create a particular outcome.

First I have to realize that there is only one constant that will be present in every situation I face for the rest of my life: *me*. I am the only *constant* that will be present in every situation that I face. This includes all of my past baggage and conditioning from my parents, friends, and society. This is what I constantly take with me everywhere I go. In Julio's case, he started with this assessment of himself: I am an extremely knowledgeable technician with years of education and apprenticeship at some top recording studios under my belt, but I am also the kind of person who feels uncomfortable drawing attention to myself.

The second element I call *improvement*. Improvement is anything I do to better myself. *Anything*. It could be as simple as a small attitude adjustment I make to acquire new skills that better prepare me to face the world, or learning as much as I can from the difficulties I have to face. Julio did as much to improve himself as time and money would allow, to the best of his ability at the time. He voraciously read books on business management, took a public speaking course through a community college program, and, through encouragement from a friend, began taking my class not only to learn how to focus through stressful situations but to interact with other people in an environment that was unfamiliar to him.

The third element of the Improved Outcome Formula is the *situation*. You have to separate yourself from it; you are not the situation. It exists independently of you—you are not responsible for the weather, for example, or for how other people choose to act. Often you put yourself in situations by volunteering to be part of something or through neglecting a responsibility. The only thing you can ultimately be responsible for in any situation is yourself. Work harder on controlling yourself than you do trying to control your situation. You will see better outcomes—as was Julio's experience. Once he accepted the fact that it is the nature of business that some people will want your product and others won't, he stopped focusing on the "what ifs" and concentrated on the known elements—his product's benefits and his experience. Selling is still something that makes him uncomfortable, but the fact is he got good enough at it to make money. The result is now he's got enough in the bank to hire someone *else* to do most of the selling.

Let me take you back to Hell Week as an example of a crappy situation: I think it was Thursday. I don't know for sure, though, because like every other enlistee I had been up for close to a hundred straight hours. The sun was going down and night was falling. We were cold, we were wet. We could barely stand up, let alone move. My legs were scabbed and cut, and my shoulders were chapped from carrying around an IBS, an inflatable rubber boat. We'd just finished chow. The instructors were mad at us and we didn't understand why, but that was nothing new. They were always mad at us for something. Suddenly the order came that we had to do push-ups with our legs angled up on the boats to increase the resistance and thus make the exercise even harder. Our arms were weak, our bodies shaking from fatigue. We were your standard cold, wet, and miserable.

This is absolutely the most miserable #*!+%! place in the world. This sucks, I kept saying over and over to myself. My arms shook. The whole thing was pathetic.

Out of nowhere I remembered advice an older navy guy had given me. He'd served for a lot of years, and I respected his opinion. He said, "Train as if they're going to kill you in BUD/S. And no matter how bad it gets, if you can find a way to put a smile on your face you'll make it through the worst. No matter what." And you know what? At that moment I did. I was there shaking but my face muscles pulled back from my lips. I bared my teeth like an animal. Then a strange thing happened: Imagining what a freakish grimace I was making made me smile for real. The next thing you know, I was thinking, Hey, I'm smiling—this is not so bad. If you instructors made it through this, I can make it through this. If you made it, *I* can make it! You had to do this, I can do this! My attitude switched from negative to positive instantly. Did my situation change at all? Not one bit. I was still in the push-up position, my legs were still cut, my arms were still tired, I still hadn't slept, the instructors were still yelling at me. Yet, everything had changed. With a slight improvement in my attitude my mind-set shifted from a fear-based perspective that this torture would never end to one where finishing was not only possible, it was guaranteed.

In ten years I can honestly say there were a lot of other times the job was much more challenging. Sometimes you think, Why the hell am I here? Why am I putting myself through this? You come to understand that a sense of humor is not only helpful, but a requirement. I was fortunate to be in platoons with men who could keep me laughing through the hell.

Chief Don Shipley was one. Imagine: You've been on an operation for three days, no food, no water, you're freezing, and you're miserable. "Crap" is too fine a word to describe how you're feeling. You could see Shipley scan us boys in his platoon, looking us up and down. Then, he looks each of us in the eye and says in a tone like he's passing hors d'oeuvres at a cocktail party, "Kick in the groin, anyone? Huh? Punch in the face? Got one left." It never failed to elicit groans and laughs. But all of a sudden, things didn't seem so bad. You knew your body could do more, you could go farther.

As long as your mind is in the game, your body is in the game. In Bukido we teach that the way to destroy an attacker is to destroy the attacker's mind. You can damage a man's body, but if you don't damage him in a way that undercuts his very thinking, he can come back. But if you destroy his mind, there's no way his body can come back. The mind is the fire. Extinguish that fire, you destroy the blaze.

I put my students in situations that provoke as much fear as possible to give them clear examples. Fear versus focus, problem versus solution. By experiencing these situations firsthand, they clearly understand which one they would rather have. The question always is, "Do you like this one better when it's full of fear? Or do you like this one when you're taking control, taking action?" Naturally, they always choose the side where the fear is nonexistent, or minimal at least.

I had a student who was deathly afraid of being choked because she had once been attacked by an abusive boyfriend. During a jealous rage he had thrown her down on the couch and held her by the throat, screaming that he would kill her. Although this had occurred more than a decade ago, she still woke up in the middle of the night with nightmares of being choked. More than that, she told me, she had grown to hate anything at all touching her neck, even a necklace.

With her consent, my assistant instructors and I put her in those exact situations she feared. Being choked is painful—I mean really painful. But it is the kind of pain you can focus through. I showed her that she could handle five seconds before she had to even take out an eye. Once she experienced this and realized she could take concrete action before her life was actually at risk, she discovered a confidence that not only helped her shake the fear of being choked, but worked as a sort of metaphor that helped her put the daily stresses of life in general in perspective. She gave me this example: "I used to freak out if I was late on some payment and got a call from a bill collector. In my mind I'd immediately go to, Oh my God, my credit is ruined, I have no future," she said. "Now I tell myself, Okay, if I can do something in five seconds when somebody is choking me, I can surely do something in a day that will make this guy ease up, too."

I often teach my students the difference between pain and chaos: You can focus through pain. In chaos, you can't. As soon as you give your thoughts away to the pain, as soon as you believe you are in chaos, you shut down.

The way to conquer fear is to move into and through it. Imagine it as a veiled, paper-thin mist and just walk through it. It's like fog: Sometimes a fog seems as dense as stone. You can't see anything through it, it seems to engulf you. But if you keep walking, putting one foot in front of the other, all of a sudden it's gone. Suddenly you can see everything. It helps some of my students to imagine fear as this paper-thin, veiled mist. And once you walk through this paper-thin mist, it's clear on the other side. Your fear is behind you.

Once students get through those artificially imposed stresses, then, hopefully, they can take that remembered experience out into the rest of their lives. It must be understood that fear is a problem. Really, nothing good comes from fear. Not better thoughts, not keener vision, not better action, not better results. Fear causes the body's natural survival mechanisms to misfire and perform unreliably. The more time it takes to recognize the fear, the longer the body and mind perform unreliably. The longer you put off addressing a problem, the harder it is to solve.

Ensuring survival comes from being able to evaluate past experiences correctly. I don't have to be a genius to evaluate when a gun is pointed at my face. Fear does not tell me, "Be smart here, this is a gun pointed at you." It's our evaluation that a gun has the potential to kill, or at the very least create massive injury, that lets us know how dicey the situation is. If I had never seen a gun before I would not understand the massive potential of this device, yet I may read the menacing body language of the individual holding the object and get a sense that something is not right. I may have seen this type of body language in an individual that has hurt me before. I might not know how this person with the device intends to hurt me, but it is clear that the intent is there. The unknown factors how, when, and why will lead to increased fear based purely on my evaluation of my past experience with this exhibited behavior.

But if you have no absolute reference to evaluate a

particular experience, the likelihood that fear will even show up decreases. That's why babies appear fearless.

"I don't buy it," one of my students, Lila, told me when I said that during a Bukido course. Lila is a systems analyst by day, and by night is a painter who at the time was about to have her first gallery opening. "I've never, ever done anything that's even remotely like showing my own work in front of an audience. But I know I'm scared of it."

"I think you have," I replied. "When you went to school did you ever have to read before the class, a book report or anything?"

"School was a long time ago, but yes," Lila said.

"Did the boys in the back row snicker? Did your teacher criticize something about the report, the way you delivered it—did she tell you to slow down, to not talk so fast?"

"I seem to remember something like that, but what are you getting at?" Lila replied.

"That you have done something like the gallery exhibit before—or at least, something your brain equates with being like the exhibit," I told her.

As adults, we have so many references based in life experience. We tend to draw conclusions from those references, and in the process we often transfer fears, appropriately and inappropriately, from situations that appear similar and fill in the gaps with images of the worst thing that could happen.

In my own experience, I have found that fear comes in two categories: uncontrolled fear and controlled fear. Uncontrolled fear rises in proportion to the number and intensity of unknowns there are—you don't know how bad it's going to be, you don't know what it's going to be, you don't know what the cause is, you don't know what the effect is, you don't know what's going to happen to you. The hands sweat, the heart races, the body shakes. In fact there are so many unknowns you can't even remember what *is* known. Thinking constricts, and your ability to solve any problem is so small that everything seems completely out of control.

Think about trying to talk to someone when a radio is playing. That's what fear is like—it's that static drowning out communication. The louder that noise is, the harder it is to hear that voice inside telling you the solution. What we want is to be able to take that fear, recognize it, move beyond it, and get a little closer to the source, actually hear what's being said to us.

Along those lines, let's say you've had a falling out with a buddy, or a coworker, or a "significant other." If your falling outs are like mine, often there's nothing but a blur of words, angry sentences thrown back and forth until you both walk away in disgust and neither of you can tell right away what exactly transpired. But after a moment—or an hour, or a few days—to sort things through, it will become evident that one or both of you reacted out of some type of fear. If you then apply the most elementary troubleshooting, it's just a problem: Working your way back through the actions and words, you can find where the fear lies and address it, if both of you are willing.

At the risk of sounding like a typical male, I have to admit that when communication breaks down in my relationships I think about it like a radio breaking down. You open it and find there are all these resistors, capacitors, transistors—things you don't know what the hell they are. Your first reaction might be, "Oh my God, I don't know what to do." Start back at the power source and work your way forward to find the chain that will eventually enable you to fix the problem.

In effect, that's what uncontrolled fear does: It shorts the connection between thought and action. What you want to do is go back to the source as quickly as possible to find a way to get around the short.

In a state of controlled fear, you have a grip on certain things—there are more things known to you than are unknown. When I jump out of the airplane I'm familiar with that event. I pump myself up beforehand to remind myself of what I know so I can go around or underneath the fears that remain—will my equipment work? Will anyone down on the ground shoot at me when I get there?

Fear is a problem, and like any problem, if you want a solution you first have to recognize that the problem exists. I believe fear is a constant in most people's lives. Fear to ask that girl out, fear to get a promotion, fear to change jobs, fear to go anywhere. We may not call it fear— we may talk about having anxiety, or being nervous, or having a general sense of unease about something, but all of these feelings are just other names for low-level fear.

It seems the biggest fear that most of us have in our daily life is the fear of looking stupid. A friend of mine in the San Bernardino Sheriff's Department once told me about a cop who failed to call for backup because he was afraid he'd look stupid to his coworkers. What happened?

He got in a firefight and got shot. That's a guy who was afraid to act based on his experience. He was afraid to act on his own knowledge. It wasn't that he was afraid of what was going to happen. He was more afraid of looking stupid than willing to be smart and calling for backup. Does that make sense? No. But it happens all the time. It's more accepted to be afraid than it is to stand up and take charge. Fear is an industry in our culture. Think about all of the people out there trying to make money off of your fear. Your fear of being fat, broke, unattractive, of being attacked, or being without someone for the rest of your life. There is enough fear out there to go insane. But more often than going insane, the culture of fear keeps us in jobs we hate, relationships that are hurtful to our self-esteem, houses we don't like, and in neighborhoods we have outgrown.

One of the biggest, and hardest, lessons I learned about fear was at SEAL Team Two, when I volunteered for a winter warfare platoon. It's one of the toughest platoons because not only is it physically demanding, but you have to put up with Arctic temperatures, sometimes 65 degrees below zero. There is never a moment where you feel warm and comfortable. I really didn't understand that when I volunteered to get into the platoon. I simply understood it was challenging, and because I was seeking mastery of myself, I wanted the challenge. I had always prided myself on the fact that if I have a fear, I always look it in the eye and walk right into it. That's really the only way you can conquer fear, because it's like a heat-seeking missile. You can't run away from it, you can't hide from it, you can't duck it. No matter where you go, it finds you. But if you walk right at it, it misses you completely. It goes right past you, as if it were just an illusion.

So imagine how difficult is was for me when I finally realized: Damn, I'm afraid of being cold. I was literally afraid of being cold, really cold. The extreme nature of Arctic temperatures can freeze appendages black, damaging them to the point where they must be amputated; basic survival is much more difficult because the environment itself could quickly kill you. It's important to remember that since I was raised in Miami, not North Dakota, I had never had the chance to become familiar with extreme cold on a day-to-day basis. Also, I had experienced cold during BUD/S and found that it has the power to grate on the mind as few things do. But as bad as that was, it never got below freezing. Being in an environment of ice and snow for months on end could only be worse by far, or so I reasoned.

But I didn't recognize this fear for a long, long time. I disguised it as anger, I disguised it as annoyance or jealousy. I even disguised it as hate sometimes. I verbally attacked people because I was afraid—I'd blow up at them and disguise my anger as a justified response to the other person's inexperience.

I remember the first time we went skiing on a downhill course. I felt like an idiot. I was overdressed because I wouldn't listen. We had hours and hours of classes before we set foot on the slopes—I'd had top-notch experts detailing for me exactly what it was I needed to do. Yet I blew off their knowledge and experience in that environment and in effect said, "Oh, I know better." But that was fear talking. It wasn't as if I had done it and found a better way to do it. No, I had never done it before in my life. Not only had I never done winter warfare before where you must navigate through avalanche terrain, shoot in hip-deep snow, and dive in glacial waters, I had never even *skied* in my entire life. But there I was, some kind of expert on knowing how to dress. All I was focused on was how to stay warm: Got to stay warm, must stay warm. But they were trying to teach me that when you're really moving out in a cold environment you can't overdress.

So I overdressed, and then I overheated, and then I sweat, and then, big surprise, I got cold. Cold surprised me—how could I be cold with so many clothes on? That caused stress in me, so I tried to compensate for that stress and that fear with very stupid thoughts. I started getting really, really uncomfortable and thinking about how uncomfortable I was rather than about the mechanics of skiing. And I started thinking about things that didn't matter versus things that did. My fear caused me to put on more and more clothing. More and more clothing caused me to overheat so I was now super-uncomfortable in an environment where I would otherwise have just been uncomfortable. And I couldn't think about any of the things I was supposed to do. I was afraid to go down the hill because I didn't know how to control my skis, because I hadn't listened to anything they'd been saying about how to get down a slope. This would have been fine if a hot toddy were waiting for me back at the lodge after a hard day on the bunny slope, but the fact of the matter was that within days I had to be ready to spend fifteen days plowing through Arctic snow and sleet with a ninety-six-pound pack strapped to my back. Imagine hearing the ice formed from your own sweat breaking off your body at the same moment you realize, I've still got twenty miles to go before I get to pitch a tent on ice. . . .

Only two things can get in the way of knocking down a target, or accomplishing a goal: lack of knowledge, or fear. That's it. If somebody teaches you how—given time to absorb new concepts and given the time needed for experiencing and training those concepts—yet you still don't do what they tell you to do, guess what: it's fear.

When I say knowledge, that includes the training and conditioning of that knowledge. Knowledge doesn't come from somebody telling you something. It's information when it's just out there. Knowledge is information you've taken on board and integrated into your decisions and actions.

Sometimes I would do it right, sometimes I would do it wrong. I couldn't get consistent because I was thinking more about things that weren't necessary versus the things that were. Eventually I picked up the mechanics for downhill skiing. I went through two and a half years fighting through fear, fighting through the knowledge that I would not accept in order to be successful. Why was it so hard? Because mentally I was not aware of my fear.

As I said, it's better to look fear in the eye right away because eventually the two of you will meet up again. I managed to force myself through the fear. Over time, as I became more familiar with the environment, there was less fear and I started subconsciously taking off a little more of the clothes. As I became more and more familiar with the environment, I started to actually respect the harshness of the landscape and it wasn't so shocking to me anymore. I still had those fears—don't get me wrong—but the interference got lighter, and so my thinking got a little clearer. And all you need is a little bit of clarity to do one thing right. The next thing you know, I started doing little things better here and there.

So when all was said and done I had managed to do a decent job, and I was given the opportunity to go to French school when I came back. Four months of sitting in a warm classroom was a welcome break—plus, by the time I got finished I could order a glass of wine and ask a French girl for her phone number.

But as soon as I came back from that, I had my new orders waiting for me.

"You're going to ski instructor school," my commanding officer told me.

The fear leapt back into my body. "I don't know anything about skiing, I'm the worst skier in the planet. Why are you guys sending me to ski instructor school? What are you, high?" I said. I mean, that's what I felt like saying. I was in the military, after all. There's not much room for discussion.

Sometimes, however, the universe has lessons to teach you and you don't have a choice. Good things can come from that. The best learning experience came from this challenge I wasn't willing to face.

So off I went, back out on the snow. And something unexpected happened. By no means was I some kind of honor student, but where the best skiers only improved on their skill by maybe 25 percent, I improved my own personal abilities by 100 percent. I managed to get an instructor's certification. Now, I wasn't skiing like somebody who'd been born with skis strapped on his feet, but for the first time I perfected the basic mechanics and correct fundamentals—how your balance works, putting your chest down the fall line—all the things I'd just muscled through before. I began saying to myself, Hey, I'm understanding this information, meaning, now it's starting to become knowledge.

Before long the class was over, and right away I had a platoon of my own to teach. And you know what? My evaluations rated me as a key instructor in the program, one "who performed flawlessly." How did I, a former idiot on skis, became one of the best instructors? Two reasons: Not only did I know correct fundamentals, I always remembered what it was like to be a beginner. And once I started finding success in one area, all of the other stuff almost instantly made sense to me.

Ultimately the more familiar you are with an environment, the less fear you have of that environment. The less fear, the less interference to being able to take on knowledge, to be able to do things. If you can learn one thing from my misery in winter warfare, understand that interference can last for *years* without you even being aware of it. You can lash out at people, you can get mad at yourself—you can even end up hating yourself without ever realizing that fear is the interference, the block in the road of progress. Fear only causes me to react. Fear only causes me to wait. *Fear moves me away from effective action.* When you find yourself acting like a jerk, stop for a second and just ask yourself, What am I afraid of here?

I truly believe there are two root emotions to everything a person experiences. You are either moving toward fear or you're moving toward love. Positive emotions, I believe, are attached to some kind of love. During my skydive where so many things went wrong, I was able to get my thoughts in control because I wanted to live through the experience. I knew I had so many things worth living for. The value I placed on my life was stronger than my fear of death.

Every time I get ready to jump out of an airplane, I feel fear. The unknown of death has inherent fear. I don't want to die. *But being afraid of dying isn't what pulls your chute. Wanting to live does.* Plenty of people commit suicide by jumping off a building. That is not wanting to live. That is wanting to jump away from life into death, that ending it somehow will be better than living it. Now, they may not be saying to themselves, I'm jumping to love, but they think they're jumping to something that has greater value than life. Maybe it is as simple as relief or revenge, or the feeling that death is somehow better than living.

All negative emotions are attached to some fear, without exception. When I wanted to be a SEAL I had fear of Hell Week. But if I would have followed that fear, let it consume me, I never would have accomplished becoming a SEAL. If I followed that fear, I never would have pulled that parachute, I never would have solved that problem. Living in fear keeps you from acting effectively. It's that simple. The more things you care about passionately in your life, the more you build inherent value in your life. The less you have of value in your life, the more you feel you're moving toward fear.

Think about this for a second: Remember when you experienced love for another person for the first time. Think about that first experience—you had unlimited energy. Unlimited. You could stay up all night talking to that person, you could run around all day, you could go through anything just to get to that person. You would do whatever is possible to get to that moment of togetherness. Think about what it would be like if we lived life like we're always falling in love.

I have a motto I always say in class: "Aggressively live life." A student helped me understand that the Latin root of the word "aggressive" means "to move toward." So when I say I live aggressively, it means I go after the experience of living. When you're doing that you're open, your energy is unlimited, and you can do anything.

Joyce was a student I met two years after she had suffered a horseback riding accident that nearly cost her her life. An experienced equestrienne who had grown up riding, Joyce was out on the trail by herself one day. She and her horse came to a hedge they had jumped many times before, but this day the footing on the other side was wet and slippery. As her horse landed, he stumbled and Joyce fell. But what happened in the next moment was worse: As he came to his feet, the horse tried to step away from Joyce, but instead his rear hoof hit her thigh, tearing through the skin, crushing her bone and cutting an artery. She was lucky someone came along and found her before she bled to death.

Although it was a long, painful road to recovery, Joyce eventually was able to get back up on her horse. At first it was just to sit while the animal walked around the ring, but eventually she felt strong enough to get back to her regular riding style. Yet, all of a sudden, fear caught up to her—her hands would shake, her throat would constrict, she couldn't focus on anything but the terror of

being injured again. She was facing uncontrolled fear—
and the more fearful she became, the more her horse
sensed something was wrong and became fearful himself.
The combined fears of the horse and rider were quickly
creating a dangerous situation.

Joyce came to me not because she thought Bukido
would help her with fear, but because she wanted to do
something that might help her improve her sense of balance. But one day she came to class and I could see she
had been crying.

"What's wrong?" I asked.

"I'm never going to be able to ride again, and that
makes me feel like a part of myself is dying," she told me,
obviously distraught.

Just the way she said that made it clear to me that her
love of horses and all the joy that had brought her was still
stronger than her fear of being hurt. After some experimen-
tation I developed for her an exercise called Fear Crusher,
which I now use for all my students. It comes in two sections:

SECTION I: PRIDE DRILL

1. *Write down a moment in your life when you felt you really accomplished something, large or small.* It doesn't matter when it happened—it could have been when you were five years old or
   just yesterday. Examples: landing a big account at work.
   Tying your shoes for the first time as a child. Running your
   first ten-mile race. Underneath that, write down as many
   things as you can about that moment that made it so special.

   Read back over what you have written. Take a moment
   to really see how those words look on paper.

2. *Write down all the things that you value about the idea of hitting your current target.* This should include: what you imagine your life would be like after accomplishing it, how you will feel about yourself, and how it might alter the way others perceive you.

 Then, turn all of those things into one powerful, motivating sentence. My motivating sentence is often, "I'm doing what I want and I know what I'm doing." I used it many times when the job called for me to do something like dive into pitch-black waters with a bomb strapped to my back.

3. *Write down three things that happen to you when you are nervous or afraid.* Examples: Do you start talking really fast? Does your stomach get tight? What are some of the things that you say to yourself? This is to help you recognize your dialogue and other telltale signs of fear when they approach.

4. *Create an action trigger.* This is a command that propels your mind and body into action. Examples: "Go for it!" "Showtime!"

SECTION II: MOVE THROUGH FEAR

1. *Recognize your telltale signs of fear.* In Joyce's case, when she was riding she would start to hunch her shoulders and look down at the ground. She found herself saying things like, "This is going to be bad," "I could come off any second," and "Oh no, this could scare my horse, he's crazy . . ."

2. *Recall the sense of accomplishment you wrote down in your Pride Drill. Feel it as if it were happening again.* I had Joyce shut her eyes and imagine what it felt like the first time she and her horse cleared a fence, how nice it was to be all dressed up

in her riding clothes and have her horse groomed, and how good it felt to be handed a ribbon.

3. *Repeat your powerful motivating sentence three times slowly.* Example: "I love this because it proves that my instincts about the market are right." "If I can do this I can do anything." Joyce would say to herself, "I love my horse, I have been a rider all my life and I can keep on riding."

4. *Calmly and simply state what it is you are going to accomplish.* Out loud if you can; firmly to yourself if others are pres-ent. Joyce didn't set a goal of riding in the Olympics, because that's not what mattered or what she was ultimately training for. Instead her goal was to connect with her horse and perform her basic routine to the best of her ability. So she said, "I am going to ride today, hit my points, stay relaxed, and have fun."

5. *Take a deep breath, hold it, let it out.*

6. *Pull your action trigger: "Showtime!" "Go for it!"* Joyce would say, "Let's do it!" and then put her foot in the stirrup.

7. *Go!!!!!!!!!* She who dares, wins. And I mean that literally: Although at first it wasn't easy, Joyce dedicated herself to getting through and beyond her fear. After six months she competed in a small, local show and took home a blue ribbon. "I thought about all the times it felt like me and my horse were the same creature and how it would feel like flying," she reported. "Then I pulled my action trigger, 'Let's do it,' and away we went! I do that every time I ride now." With practice this process will get easier, require less energy, and take less time. Like Joyce, you'll eventually be able to do it all in seconds.

This chapter has been about understanding the nature of fear, how and why it shuts down your decision-making ability. Unless fear is acknowledged as the problem it is, it will always lead you back to the same place—and there you'll be, not understanding why the targets you've set up remain so hard to knock down. I've provided you with a few tools to dissipate fear, but let's now begin to create a way of being that continually moves you through fear and beyond it toward your targets.

Chapter 3

Create an Action Mind-set

Act as though it were impossible to fail.
—*Winston Churchill*

What is an Action Mind-set? It's the state of mind you need to have in order to handle any situation. It's formed by the language we use to talk to ourselves, and even slight changes in the words we choose can have a significant impact on our actions. I'm going to give you an example of this. The more fully you participate in imagining this scene, the more you'll get out of it.

It's getting dark, and you've just pulled into your driveway. You're tired from a long, busy day at work. All you want to do when you get inside is kick your shoes off, relax on the sofa, and watch a little TV. You walk up to your front door, unlock it, and enter your house. After you have stepped inside you turn, close the door, and lock it. It's dark inside your entryway and you reach to flip on the light switch on the wall near the window. By the moonlight shining in, you suddenly see a large man coming at you with a baseball bat in his hand.

He wants to hurt *you,* so you get ready to *defend yourself.*

Now you see him raise the bat and begin to swing. *You throw your hand up and cover your face.*

Stop.

How did that make you feel? Were you anxious? Was it painful to imagine? What happened to your arm? Did feelings of helplessness rise?

Let's try it again.

It's getting dark, and you've just pulled into your driveway. You're tired from a long, busy day at work. All you want to do when you get inside is kick your shoes off, relax on the sofa, and watch a little TV. You walk up to your front door, unlock it, and enter your house. After you have stepped inside you turn, close the door, and lock it. It's dark inside your entryway and you reach for the light switch on the wall near the window. By the moonlight shining in, you suddenly see a large man coming at you with a baseball bat in his hand.

He wants to hurt *you,* so you decide to *take him out.*

Now you see him raise the bat and begin to swing. *You throw your hand up and bury your fingers in his eye. The bat falls from his hand. He yelps and stumbles to the ground.*

Stop.

Now, how does that make you feel?

This is the Reactive versus Active Mind scenario I put my students through in the beginning of their training. If you are like each and every one of them, you found that in the second scenario you felt in control—you might have even had the sensation of feeling physically larger. I teach this concept to Bukido students before they learn any physical moves. I come into the room, put my assistant instructor in front of them, and shout, "Get ready to defend yourselves!" without telling them how or what to do. The universal response is to jump backward, hunch the shoulders, and put hands in the air. The students who have previous martial arts experience might do this smoothly and calmly, the sixty-year-old banker might do it awkwardly, but all of them, without exception, physically retract in some way.

Then I shout, "Take him out!" Immediately their body language changes—they are propelled forward, hands out, moving straight at the person in front of them. Even if they don't know what they are doing, they physically throw their bodies forward. It's like somebody just grabbed them by a rope and yanked them forward. One command freezes them, the other unleashes them.

It's one of the most important things anybody walks away with from Bukido training. You can hear it until you go deaf, but the things you say to yourself really do make a difference in how you live. You can read it in a hundred magazines or books, but when you have a visceral experience of it, there's no arguing: Internal dialogue affects external performance.

Let me take you back to my struggles with winter warfare training. The first time I went down a slope all I could think was, I can't get my skis to work. If you're focused on being out of control, are you focused on being *in* control? Obviously not. I brought that thought into reality very quickly, because I gave my discipline away by thinking about being out of control. Also, I was afraid of looking stupid—that universal fear we talked about in the last chapter. Think about it. I had been in the martial arts for a long time, been a SEAL for a fair number of years. I felt pretty confident on my feet, pretty good with my balance. And then I got in a new environment, a completely alien environment, and I felt like an adolescent. I feared I would look dumb; my dialogue inside told me, These guys think I'm a moron because I can't do this stuff. I kept feeding myself that dialogue, and, big surprise, I kept becoming that dialogue. The reality was the skis worked fine—it was *me* that wasn't working.

Now that you recognize fear, I'm going to give you a few tools that will help you intensely focus your thinking so that you can act effectively no matter what the situation. This two-pronged program creates an action-oriented thought process so that you can teach yourself to use commands that propel you into practical action. Just as the scenario above illustrates, you may act, but that action can be useless or, at worst, detrimental. Learn to move in a direction that will get you somewhere.

Creating an Action Mind-set begins with understanding what I call *verbal-influence conditioning.* Words influence our minds and condition our actions. The words you use generate the direction in which you go mentally and physically. Verbal-influence conditioning lets you take an aggressive and systematic approach to your "self-talk" that

will get things done. It begins with knowing what words
you habitually tell yourself, and what value you give them.

We all respond to self-talk in a similar way. If I'm six
feet five and weigh 335 pounds, play for the NFL, make $4
million a year, and say, "I'm worthless, I hate myself," I am
going to start creating self-destructive behavior—like drug
or alcohol abuse, blowing off important appointments,
mishandling money, cultivating friends in low places—just
exactly the same as if I were a five feet two, 110-pound college girl who's saying those identical things to herself. It's
just that college girls engaging in self-destructive behavior
don't make for spectacular headlines or great segments
on *ESPN SportsCenter*, so we often have the impression that
somebody famous destroying his life is a unique phenomenon. But, in fact, it's not.

You have to become distinctly aware of the words you
choose to say to yourself, and what verbal-influence conditioning you're creating. I'm no psychoanalyst, so I can't
tell you how you started calling yourself smart, or fat, or
good with your hands, or never good enough—or whatever, take your pick. But, I have discovered this for myself:
*The fact that we can change our feelings means we have power
over them.* And if this is true, it is also true that we have to
understand that being in charge of our feelings means we
can't blame them on anybody else. Start changing your
feelings by challenging your assumptions about what you
think of yourself. Whenever you hear that voice in the
back of your head say, "I can't," ask the questions: Where
is the evidence that I can't? Is this literally true? Has anyone else been able to do this? In other words, don't
believe everything you hear, even if you are the one doing
the talking.

One of the best lessons I ever had in this began as a friendly outing one night in Southeast Asia with a few of my SEAL teammates and a group of Korean "ROK" marines. We had just finished an amphibious landing that had involved a couple of long, cold, wet nights and some serious demolitions that created plumes of water reaching hundreds of feet in the air. We were kicking back at a beachfront bar—actually, it was a tiny shack with sand for a floor, bamboo for walls, and dried palm fronds for a ceiling. I swear, it looked like something out of *Gilligan's Island.*

Who knows how these things get started, but somehow the subject came up about the tough reputation Americans have, or think they have.

"Your president is a Hollywood cowboy," joked our Korean counterparts. "You are all show."

"Think so?" said Tony. He was smiling, but it didn't matter. Tony always looked mean. He was the kind of guy who had to duck and walk sideways through doorjambs because his shoulders wouldn't fit. There weren't a lot of people in this world who would, or could, tell Tony what to do.

"See this guy right here?" Tony pointed in my direction, so I looked over my shoulder to see who he was pointing at. Nobody was there. It had to be me he was talking about.

He walked over and put his hand on my shoulder. "Mack can beat your best guy at arm wrestling. And he won't even break a sweat."

I looked up at Tony and thought, Are you insane? What are you doing? But I would no sooner say that than I would jump in front of a moving train—unless the job called for it and I had practiced it a few times.

The Koreans started laughing and raising their

beers. To them I was the skinny little new guy in the corner, weighing in at maybe 165 pounds. I was the "nice
guy," the one who acted polite and learned to say "please"
and "thank you" in their language. "That's a good one,"
they joked. "We'll bet you a round."

"You're on," Tony said, a wide, knowing grin spread-
ing across his face.

I sat down on one of the wooden stools and over walks
what I can only describe as the Hulk: 215 pounds—huge
for an average Korean—thick and solid as concrete. He
smiled but it was more like a snarl. "Let me put you out of
your misery, shrimp," he said—or words to that effect.

Tony leaned down and put his hand on the back of
my neck, commanding my full and complete attention.
"Remember," he said slowly in low, even tones, "you are a
SEAL."

I knew what he meant. He meant win. He meant that
my actions represent the most elite corps created in the
history of the American military. He meant every inch of
my being had to be dedicated to excellence, to a level of
supreme effort most people never demand of themselves.
"You are a SEAL" equals a kind of armor. When you are in
the heat of battle you don't feel the armor, but when you
are just sitting around on a barstool on a beach with it on
and you just want to relax, sometimes you think, This feels
a little heavy today . . .

I turned back around to the Hulk. We put our hands
together. His palm was wider and it enveloped mine. I
kept repeating, "I am a SEAL" to myself, then finally let
the words escape my lips in a whisper.

"Go!"

And then it was on. I could feel the force of the Hulk's arm bearing down. I pulled something up from inside me and before he even had time to blink, his hand was slammed down against the rough wood. He looked startled, then the look shifted to defeat. He knew he'd have a lot of explaining to do to his corpsmates that night about how a scrawny American kid on his first platoon managed to get the better of him. I wonder if he would have taken it better if he'd realized it wasn't the puny Miami kid who'd beaten him. It was the Navy SEAL in me who did it.

I see the exact opposite happen with people all the time. Jake was severely injured in a motorcycle accident a few years ago, and as a consequence a few areas of his body are weaker than others. One shoulder was also dislocated, so it is structurally weaker than the other and his ankle was crushed, requiring extensive surgery. During one class he was in the middle of a target-training combination when he went for the eye strike to his training partner. Jake then was about to move in for the follow-up kick to the groin when I saw him hesitate and make a stutter step. I could see the second-guessing going on in his brain loud and clear, as if he had a billboard over his head.

"What happened?" I asked. "I could see you were thinking about something other than the target."

"I don't know," he said. "I just got flustered."

"You were about to kick with your bad leg, right?"

"Yes," he admitted.

"There are only three things that could be going on if you are not thinking about the target," I told him. "You could be thinking about how much pain it will cause if you make contact with that leg. You could be worried that when you put your leg down after you have kicked him that you will lose your balance. Or, maybe you are not clear about what weapon you are trying to use."

"You forget where I'm at, Richard," he replied. "Major bones and ligaments were destroyed in my ankle. I am more or less walking around thanks to a bunch of titanium pins that hold my joint together."

It became clear to me that his verbal-influence conditioning was telling him "I'm injured, I'm limited." We needed to replace the old conditioning with new conditioning that would allow Jake to see everything he could do rather than the few things he couldn't. I replied, "I understand that. The physical mechanisms literally aren't there for you to develop control, but let's use what you do have. You have to make your capabilities exceed your limitations."

So instead of using the shin of his leg, he used his knee. He learned to swing his fist as though he were bowling for the groin, and how he could stomp through a knee without overextending himself. He also learned how to strike targets from different angles while on the ground. Jake was now thinking about the things he could do, rather than dwelling on all the things that he could not. His self-talk was now moving in a productive way.

Paul had a problem that was more subtle. Unlike Jake, who was injured in a motorcycle accident, he had no physical impairment—in fact, he was a natural athlete. In his first lesson he picked up the physical discipline of Bukido with greater ease than almost anyone I've taught. Paul was a smart person, a high school grad with a few years of community college to his credit. He was a talented artist with a real gift for special effects makeup, and that had always been his dream job. But at age thirty-four, he was still working in a job that paid just slightly more than minimum wage and lived in a tiny apartment with a long-standing girlfriend. They'd been going out for nearly seven years but no one could understand why, since they rarely were heard to say a civil word to each other.

I couldn't figure out what the deal was with Paul—why did he choose to do so little when he had so much he could be doing with the artistic gift he'd been given? So I started paying closer attention to the things Paul said in class. Sure enough, the same words kept coming out of his mouth, things like "whatever," "good enough," and "no way." More than once I heard him talk about liking a new car, or admiring a beautiful woman at the gym, then he'd add with a smirk and a shrug of his shoulders, "Yeah, like *that* would ever happen. . . . " They seemed like throwaway phrases in casual conversation, harmless habits of speech. In fact, they were much more than that: They indicated a verbal-influence conditioning that said that no matter what, failure was inevitable, that what he had was all he was ever going to get, and that the fulfillment of dreams only happened to other people.

I hoped Paul would glean information from class that would help him understand the ways he sabotaged his own desires, but after a few classes Paul's attendance became irregular, and soon, like he had done with other things in his life, Paul just faded out before he could even see the simplest results from training. Some months later I ran into him in a mall.

"That was cool stuff I learned in your class," he offered after we'd said our hellos.

"Yeah? Great," I said with a smile. "So what are you up to?"

"Well, there is somebody who was thinking about starting a makeup school and thought maybe I could teach something, but I don't think that's really going to pan out," he told me. "My dad wants me to move back to Washington to work in his gravel business, so if things don't start taking off I could do that. . . . My girlfriend thinks I should get a degree and maybe do some paralegal work, but I don't know . . . "

"What do you want to do, Paul?" I asked.

He shrugged. "I'm not sure."

"Sounds like you need to pick a target," I began, but I could see his gaze was already turning away. I patted him on the shoulder. "Never mind, man. Great to see you. Good luck."

I find that it can be difficult to identify the verbal-influence conditioning that's working against you. To help ferret it out so you can transform it into something positive, I use this exercise:

Your mission, should you choose to accept it: Keep a journal for three days straight, recording your thoughts throughout the day. Write down as much as you can. If you have to do this on Friday, Saturday, and Sunday when work pressures aren't usually so intense, then do it. However, you will get your best results if you do this for three consecutive days during the week. The reason for this is simple: You face more challenges during the workweek than on the weekend. And remember to be ruthlessly honest with yourself. Write down the thoughts as they come to you. Don't edit them while you write them down. The only person *you cheat* by editing your thoughts is *yourself.*

Don't give yourself an out. If you do, you'll use it when things get tough!

After you have completed this exercise, get two different color highlighter markers. Highlight, in one color, all of the negative verbal-influence conditioning that you find in your journal, then highlight all positive entries that you find in the other color.

This exercise, honestly completed, will show you not only what you think about yourself and your surroundings, but how you communicate with yourself. The quality of your internal dialogue determines the quality of your exterior performance. The challenge now is to take control of the dialogue you use with yourself. Every month do this exercise again to monitor your improvement or lack of improvement. Don't be too hard on yourself—you've got a lifetime of conditioning to overcome. After all, it took twenty years for the first episode of *Star Wars* to show up.

To help you replace any unproductive verbal-influence conditioning you might be carrying around—and let's face it, everybody does—feel free to use any one or all of the elements from *Bukido's Code of the Warrior Spirit*™. Repeat this to yourself instead of habitual phrases you use that could be holding you back:

1. I will be responsible for my life and my actions.
2. I will concentrate all the energy of my body and mind on *one* specific target at a time.
3. I will develop the ability to remain calm and composed, for even in the worst situations I will find opportunity.
4. I will spend my time wisely, for it is too precious a commodity to waste.

5. I will continually challenge myself to learn by exposing myself to others with skills greater than my own.
6. I will develop patience in all things, for it is the essential quality of a powerful mind.
7. I will make my capabilities exceed my limitations.

After you get a handle on the verbal-influence conditioning that underlies your behavior in general, you can most effectively use what in Bukido is known as the *Verbal Command Request*™ (or VCR). The Verbal Command Request is a command you give yourself or another person. It has to be structured in a way that will elicit a specific result. Nike has built one of the most successful advertising campaigns around a Verbal Command Request: "Just Do It."

Action Mind-set: The process of recognizing and moving beyond your fear to completely focus on the knowns. The process begins by understanding the words we use that influence our thoughts and condition our actions.

Verbal Command Request: A command you use on yourself or another that is structured in a specific way to elicit a known result.

My understanding of this evolved from little phrases, mantras really, that would pump me up when the going got tough. On missions I would tell myself, I am going to get home if it's the last thing I do on this planet. There were times when I was keenly aware of the fact that the only thing between me and certain death was a piece of equipment, or a buddy covering my back, and for those times what drove me and kept me on track was this loop that kept repeating in my head: "I can only be defeated in two ways, if I give up or die." This brings the mind into the task that has to be accomplished, intensifies the desire to make it a reality, and thus propels the body to action. I wrote that down in pencil on a little scrap of paper and carried it around so long that the words faded off the paper, but I still knew what they said.

Later I discovered that by making a Verbal Command Request shorter you increase the imperativeness of the command, and that creates the driving intensity necessary to bring that action into existence even more quickly. *The simpler the command, the easier it is to remember and the easier it is to recall under extreme stress.* My brother, John, is the one who helped me realize this. I had just gotten out of the navy and he was asking me about my winter warfare experiences. I was telling him some of the mental games I played with myself to get through it.

"That kind of reminds me of when you were a kid," he said suddenly. "Remember that thing you used to say?"

"That I wanted to go out with each of Charlie's Angels?" I laughed.

"Still dreamin', huh? No, idiot, you used to say 'Pain to power,' " he replied. "You remember that? We would get into fights, I would hit you a few times, and you would start whispering this 'pain-to-power' thing. I would start slugging you really good but nothing had any effect on

you. Eventually you would punch me in the face, and if I
was lucky, Mom would walk in and break it up. I remember thinking that nothing could hurt you."

"Well, in the last ten years I found a few things that
could hurt . . . " I joked, but I was already remembering
what a powerful little phrase that was for me. Literally, it
meant to me that for every punch that landed I got
stronger from it, and meaner, and tougher. Pain meant I
was still in the game, and had a chance to win.

So "I can only be defeated in two ways, if I give up or
die" was shortened to, "Not dead, can't quit." That was the
shorthand for the conversation I would have with myself:
"Are you dead yet?"

"No."

"Then don't quit."

The extreme nature of the command made things
very clear-cut for me. Giving up then became a choice,
and therefore instantly recognizable. That single statement allowed me to get through a decade of the most
intense SEAL training—and has effectively guided me
through the rest of my life.

For us in SEAL Team, work was only over once we
were physically back home. The conventional wisdom said
that the operation wasn't over until we were actually back
in the showers at home. Up until that point, nothing could
be taken for granted. When you are going toward your
extraction point after you have taken out your primary target, you can get ambushed on the way home. Once back,
when you're cleaning your gear, putting everything away so
that you are set up for the next mission, you could have a
loaded round in your weapon and accidentally shoot your-

self or someone else through carelessness or lack of attention. There were times I was so dog-tired after a twenty-hour day in the field, I had to fight the call of sleep during that final half hour it would take to clean my M14. It was a chore that I would have loved to have blown off were it not for the fact that my training drilled into me the fact that a professional doesn't quit until every task is complete. The "It ain't over until you're in the shower" phrase the BUD/S instructors used instilled in all of us a sense of follow-through and hypervigilance. To keep myself awake and on track I'd ask myself, Are you in the shower?

In your everyday life you aren't—God willing—going to have a grenade launched or a semiautomatic round fired at you, but if you have created your own VCR it can help you build a follow-through mentality so you'll always know what direction you are headed in and develop the momentum that you need to follow through to the end objective. That momentum makes it possible for you to knock down the hurdles along the path that get in the way of your targets.

One of my students is a perfect example. She comes from a rough-and-tumble family from the Allegheny Mountains of western Pennsylvania, and she herself is no shrinking violet. She's now a successful screenwriter, but struggled for years to break into professional writing. She had so many rejection letters she used them as wallpaper in her guest bathroom! When I asked what kept her going through years of discouragement, she told me, "There's an expression in my family, 'Your grandmother was a Wilcox, and a Wilcox fights.' Old Grandma Wilcox was famous for raising six kids, fighting with the tax assessor and winning, and doing a whole bunch of other near-mythic feats. It means that no matter how rotten things get, you not only can keep going, you *have* to keep going, because that's the way you're made. I just kept telling myself, Grandma was a Wilcox." That family expression had turned into a powerful Verbal Command Request, demanding action even in the face of failure.

You can structure specific physical actions, coordination, and movement all with a super-short VCR. We do this in Bukido. All the physical mechanics, particular weapons, locations in time and space, burning intensity, and complete commitment are driven solely by a target. That target is then given a label, and that label becomes a preloaded "action trigger." For example, when I tell a student "eyes" after he has perfected the mechanics of an eye strike, the word unleashes him toward his target. I spend a lot of time developing every element of the strike, and for a while it requires detailed explanation every time the students do it, but as their skills increase I start saying less and less. A little time passes and I say even less. Then all I say is "eyes." And eventually all they do is *think* it, and they can do everything.

Likewise, the same idea applies to structuring specific mental connections and verbal communication, all with a super-short command. Here's an example of what I mean: Let's say you and your significant other often have arguments over a particular subject. Perhaps you don't agree on political issues, so any time the news comes on you two end up in a spat over the president's policy in China. The fact is you probably knew your partner had radically different views on politics before you deepened your relationship—so, ultimately, how he or she votes wasn't the most important issue in the relationship. Arguing about the president's policy in China over the dinner table sure isn't going to change the policy and it's certainly not going to bring the two of you any closer. When you find yourself revving up to "set them straight," stop for a second and think, Is hammering my point home worth sacrificing the harmony of the moment? Create a Verbal Command Request like "Harmony," or "Chill" to say to yourself. Make it something that will remind you that the target of this relationship is compatibility, and thereby soften your language—both your body language and the words you say.

For a Verbal Command Request to work, you need to be very specific about what you want it to accomplish. It has to bring back that same intensity every single time you use it. Try a couple out, find the one that works the best. Remember, it only has to make sense to you—"Grandma was a Wilcox" doesn't say much to me, but it certainly doesn't stop it from being a meaningful command to my screen-writing student that kept her writing even when she had no encouragement that her words would find an audience.

You'll find that Verbal Command Requests not only work on yourself but can also work on other people as well. When I first started teaching those rape prevention semi-nars to women, I was trying to design a command struc-ture that appeared to be a request but in actuality was a command. If a woman orders an attacker to "Go away," there's a chance it will inflame him even further, and make him want to "show her who's boss" even more.

However, if she says "Please go away," even in the same harsh tone, it softens the command without taking away any of the imperativeness. You don't have to mean "please," but because even the worst cretins are conditioned to the word "please," we are more likely to hear the word "please" first, then swallow easier what is commanded afterward. "Please go away" is then heard more as a request, but in fact it is not. This helps a woman draw a line in the sand so that if this man comes any closer, there is no doubt he is a threat, and she must act on her plan. Although I initially intended it for women, I have found that in civilian society, it works for everyone, men, women, young, old.

I often ask students why they think one person ever attacks another person. I get all kinds of responses: "Because he was locked in a closet as a child," or "Because he is trying to intimidate someone else," or "Because he wants what you have," or "Because he has no other way to vent his aggression." They are all wrong. There is only one reason anybody ever attacks anybody else—whether it's on the street or in a bar or across the conference room table: *Because they think they can.* Period.

It's just that simple. Their belief that they think they can gives them all the permission they need to start their attack. This has nothing to do with whether they have the skills or ability to see the attack through. One of my clients owns a computer hardware company, and she also happens to be a very attractive woman in her forties—a detail I mention only because it seems to be an issue in the male-dominated world of technology. She tells the story of being on one business trip to negotiate a purchase of material used in the production of her product: She arrived a little early for a meeting and was alone with a buying agent for the other company, a low-level manager. After what seemed like a cordial greeting, the man, in the most condescending manner imaginable, proceeded to "explain" to her that the discussion would likely involve "a lot of technical terms" that "might be too much for her to follow," and he implied he was the one who would be calling the shots, so to speak, on the particulars of the sale.

"What I got from his conversation was he thought since I was there early I was there to take notes for my boss, who had yet to arrive. He assumed I was an easy mark for his little power play," she tells. "I can't even describe the look on his face when his boss walked in and told him I was not only the buyer and the president of the company, but the inventor of the product being manufactured!" The man was not in a position to call the shots in this situation, but when he looked at this woman, he made a series of wrong assumptions and condescended to her simply because he thought he could.

After you establish a Verbal Command Request, you have drawn a line in the sand. If the person crosses that, there is no doubt you are being attacked, a boundary has been crossed, and now you must act. Try it on a telemarketer and you'll see what I mean: If a telemarketer calls and introduces himself, tell him, "Sorry, not interested." If he keeps talking, say, "Don't call me again." If he keeps talking, that's your cue to hang up. It's a simple plan, but the principles behind it work nearly every time you face an unsolicited confrontation. Remember to keep your commands short and in bite-size chunks. This keeps you focused on your agenda, not on theirs.

It's the bad guy's tendency to go after an easy mark. Remember, they chose you because they think they can take you. I mean, why does the old saying go "You always hurt the one you love"? Because you can—usually without fear of a surprise reprisal. Sad, but true.

Each time I'd run into my neighbor, Jacob, he would spend a good ten minutes giving me the latest installment of a continuing drama at his work. The sous chef at a ritzy L.A. restaurant, Jacob felt picked on by the executive chef. "We can be talking about something banal and, out of the blue, he'll start attacking me," Jacob told me more than once.

My question was always, "What does he attack you about?"

"Anything! It doesn't matter if it's my responsibility or not. It can be about how fresh the salmon is, or the late bread delivery. Now at work I feel panicked all the time, never knowing when the chef is going to set off the next bomb!"

Despite Jacob's belief to the contrary, conflicts don't arise out of nowhere. In my experience I have found that four elements precede any conflict. Once you identify them, you can be aware of them, no matter how subtle or quickly they take place:

PRELUDE TO A CONFLICT

1. *The Pitch*: This is the first moment you are confronted with a potential adversary. It can be direct or indirect.

The direct pitch is something like a fixed stare; he wants me to make a decision one way or another. It's a sizing up. It could be, "You got a problem with me?" "Hey babe, you look good in those pants." "What's the time?" Pitches should feel uncomfortable—but they don't always. The big thing with the pitch is to recognize *whether it belongs or it doesn't belong*. It might be the timing of the actions or words that seems off, or they might feel out of context for the conversation or the situation. Of the four factors, it can be the hardest to spot. From the way Jacob described his situation at work, it seemed that any time the chef didn't approach him with a direct order—in other words, when it just seemed like "normal" conversation—there was a pitch buried in his words. The chef seemed like the kind of person who didn't "chat," but used seemingly idle conversation to find something he could pick a fight about.

2. *The Warning*: The warning could be a supposedly "friendly" stranger *insisting* on helping a woman with her groceries: "You don't want to do that, let me help you with those." It can be as blatant as, "I'm warning you, I'll knock your block off if you take that parking space." Warnings are usually transmitted by body language, such as a finger being pointed, one person closing the distance to the other person. In Jacob's case the chef would start to talk more quickly and his face would take on a hawkish quality. The warning serves two purposes, either to scare you off or pump up the aggressor so he can move to the next step of a conflict, which is the standoff.

3. *The Standoff*: Think of this in the classic bar fight scenario: face to face, nose to nose, like two bucks going at it. The

standoff with my girlfriend usually goes this way: Her: "Okay, Okay, Fine. Be that way," or Me: "Fine. Go for it. Do what you've got to do." For poor Jacob it usually went something like this: Chef: "What did you just say?" Jacob: "Nothing." It's a point of tension that is *the prelude to action.*

4. *Crossing the line*: Something happens, and there will be repercussions. For Jacob it was always that his boss would start screaming, and he would be told to "get the hell out."

One person is going to be the cause, the other one is going to be the effect. This is where the attacker pulls the woman into the car, or the boss takes credit for your idea at the staff meeting. It's the point where the little boy takes his ball home and won't play with the other kids, or the point where the right hook lands squarely on someone's jaw.

I designed this mental checklist so that I could control the destination of a conflict to my advantage. Does it work all the time? Only if you don't get caught up in the dialogue of the moment. When you are more concerned with coming across as mean, or witty, or superior you become ensnared in the event, and you are not able to see it clearly. Jacob and I talked about these four elements during our neighborly talks. Understanding his boss's subtle clues helped Jacob keep his head down and work relatively untouched long enough to get another job and get the hell away from the volatile chef. He wasn't able to change the chef into a nice guy, but he was able to control himself (not this situation) so that the outcome of the chef's behavior affected him less.

There might be times, though, when you want a Verbal Command Request to escalate the emotional level of a situation. For instance, if you're in sales for a living, the chances are good you don't want to sit around all day with prospective clients shooting the breeze. You need to find out if they are really committed to doing business, and if so, how much they are able to spend. In that case you will set up a series of Verbal Command Requests as markers for conversation.

Let's take an example from my brother, John, who has worked in car dealerships. He has come to the conclusion that there are only two types of people who walk into a car business: shoppers and buyers. It's hard to turn a shopper into a car buyer, yet it's very easy to turn off a buyer and make him a shopper! The target is selling a car, so when he's faced with prospective buyers John runs through a series of VCRs to direct the conversation:

✦ "Is there a type of vehicle I can help you with?" This may seem like just a friendly request, but what it's actually doing is helping John establish their interest right off the bat, and asking them to actively engage his services. Immediately if the prospective buyer says, "I'm just looking," John knows instantly where he stands. Now John will approach him as a shopper. If the buyer says, "I like this one here," John knows the person is here for a specific vehicle.

✦ "How long have you been looking at a vehicle like this?" From this response John gets quite a few indicators of the person's level of seriousness. If the prospective buyer says his friend has one exactly like it and loves it, that tells John the person is very serious. John now knows he is moving closer to rather than away from a sale. If the prospective buyer says he has been looking for three weeks at various models but likes this one the best, he just told

John he is closer to purchase than he is to continuing his shopping. Either way, John might now suggest a test drive to strengthen the rapport with the prospective buyer. However, if he says he has been looking for three weeks and wants to do more research, John knows to approach him as someone who is not buying today but as someone whom he may see again later if he treats him right. That lets John know he should not spend a lot of time trying to wrap up a sale today.

✦ During the test drive, John will now use a third Verbal Command Request: "When you bought your last car, what was that experience like?" The answer to this gives John a clearer and better rapport with the person, and the information he needs to best handle working the negotiation process with the buyer. If the buyer says it was a great experience, John asks what made it that way. He now has a blueprint of how he, too, will conclude this negotiation. If the person reports a terrible previous experience, John knows what to avoid or to reduce the intensity of negotiation.

✦ "Would you like to have a cup of coffee or a soda and look at the numbers?" The buyer's response will be the most telling in terms of how immediate the sale will be. It will tell John if they are interested in buying a car this minute or if they need a little more time. By using these VCRs, John uses his time efficiently; instead of spending forty minutes to one hour with a customer who ultimately does not purchase, he now needs to invest only twenty minutes to determine whether a customer is a buyer or shopper. This way John visits with more customers per day, increasing his opportunities for commissions.

From the responses to Verbal Command Requests like these, you can actively drive a prospective client in one direction or the other. The beauty of this is that you know what lies ahead in each direction. The client always feels he has the choice, but you have preselected the options. This severely limits your surprise along the way.

Thinking reactively has an inherent quality of fear. People who think this way are always one step behind, trying to counter moves that have already taken place. Reactive thinking requires that you begin to think about what you're going to do and how you're going to do it only after an event has already begun to take place. How can you be anything but one step behind, scrambling to catch up, if someone else is already taking effective action and knows where they are going next? This is why in Bukido we say, It all comes down to who can cause chaos first and capitalize on it. An action mind-set is one where all your knowledge is preloaded and just waiting for you to pull the trigger and go.

Now let's move through the action mind-set using an example most everybody knows too well—the process of finding a better job.

MOVING THROUGH THE ACTION MIND-SET

1. *Pick* your target. The target is based on parameters that *you* set. You may want a position that will pay you more money, provide a bigger challenge to your abilities, stimulating you to learn and improve, and either be closer to home so there's less of a commute, or offer more flexible hours.

2. *Recognize* your fear. You might doubt your abilities, feel that security at your old place may be jeopardized if you start looking for another post, even dread the prospect of having to meet new people and carve out a new niche for yourself. There's an old saying that the devil we know is better than the devil we don't, and that applies to jobs, too.

3. *Understand* the verbal-influence conditioning that works against your desire for a new and better position. Use the exercise on page 78. Once you recognize it, you can alter it to work for you.

4. *Deploy* a Verbal Command Request to put yourself in gear and get going.

5. *Move through* and beyond whatever fear comes up. Use the exercises from chapter 2 as a guide.

6. *Completely focus* on your known action. That means once you have defined exactly what it is you're supposed to do to knock down your target, do it. Check job listings, send out resumés, contact friends to get the word out—do whatever it is you have to do. Let nothing get in the way.

We live in a world where we can't control everyone and everything, so as a result there are times when, no matter how effectively we employ an Action Mind-set, we are going to be caught in a position where we are forced to react. Take, for instance, interviewing for that new job, or for a promotion. In this situation, you will want to come across your best in an environment that is potentially stressful, and in the worst-case scenario, outright hostile. You'll have to stay flexible and competent in an interview, even though you must react to a variety of different questions and conditions. Given that, here are seven Keys to

Minimizing Reaction Time that SEALs are taught while training for counterterrorist operations:

SEVEN KEYS TO MINIMIZING REACTION TIME

1. **Limit your responses.**

   Don't try to do or say too much at one time. Keep your answers simple and to the point.

2. **Simpler techniques are faster techniques.**

   A high-pressure situation like a job interview is not the time to experiment. By keeping your answers simple and to the point, the interviewers find your point easier to follow and faster to understand.

3. **Practice your techniques (perfect practice makes for a performance you can rely on).**

   Before your interview, practice answering some of the questions you believe they might ask. Simplify your answers to the best of your abilities, saying them over and over again so they sound smooth and automatic. Develop some specific questions of your own to ask the interviewer.

4. **Position yourself so that your actions are natural, smooth, and efficient.**

   The better prepared you are for your interview, the easier it will be to stay flexible, open, and relaxed.

5. **Remember, you can react later with a fast (simple) technique than earlier with a slow (complicated) technique.**

   If you are asked a question in which you feel forced to react, take a moment to carefully consider what is being asked. Don't just blurt an answer out to fill the void of silence. If you do, you will most likely spend a considerable amount of time trying to explain what it is that you blurted out and why. By taking a moment, you will be able to give an answer that is carefully considered in less time than the one that is blurted out and has to be explained.

6. **Anticipate correctly and gain a little, anticipate incorrectly and lose a lot.**

   The more information you can gather about the particular interviewing process, the better prepared you will be to handle yourself, the interviewers, and their questions. A little piece of good information can give you an edge in the interview. Bad or incorrect information can lead you to make numerous faulty assumptions that could cost you the position you seek. I can tell you in the military, good intelligence always works toward making an operation successful.

7. **All reaction time is shortened with advance information.**

   The more homework that you do before the interview, the easier and faster it will be for you to react to what is asked of you in the interview.

There is a formula that has been in use for thousands of years: cause and effect. The ancient Chinese general and philosopher Sun Tzu used it in 400 B.C., and it works better than ever today. The Action Mind-set is a "life stance" for going forward in the world in a way where you can act effectively, no matter what's in front of you. Remember that in a warrior's mind, it is better to be the cause of an effect than to be an effect that was caused.

Chapter 4

The Four Critical Keys to Conquering Anything

> Know your enemy and yourself, and in one thousand battles you will never be in peril. When you are ignorant of the enemy but know yourself, your chances of winning or losing are equal. If ignorant both of your enemy and of yourself, you are certain, in every battle, to be in peril.
>
> —*Sun Tzu,*
> The Art of War

I want to tell you a story about my client Karen, the computer hardware manufacturer I mentioned in the previous chapter. A scientist with two Ph.Ds., Karen had invented a certain computer component designed to save money in the computer manufacturing process, while at the same time increasing the machine's computing efficiency. Excited by the breakthrough technology, a major electronics firm in Texas called for a meeting with her company to discuss the product. If they liked what they heard, the firm was prepared to set up an account that would mean more than $2 million for Karen's company.

The next Monday, Karen and two of her top managers were in a boardroom in Texas to present her product to the men from the firm—technical representatives, purchasing managers, and a vice president. Karen enthusiastically began to lay out the technical improvements inherent in her design. But something was terribly wrong.

While they smiled at her politely, some were doodling on their notepads, some were holding their brows, some were even whispering among themselves. In short, they were doing everything but paying attention to what she had to say. When the men did have questions, they didn't ask her but rather directed their queries to her production manager, Peter.

Karen initially felt a burst of anger. "How *dare* they treat me this way," she fumed. "It's the same old crap. They don't believe a woman can know this much about what they do!" But she knew if this situation got away from her, so would a two-million-dollar account. She had to think of a way to turn this situation to her favor, because otherwise she was going down in flames. And fast.

You understand that the target dictates the weapon and the weapon dictates the movement, that fear interferes with your decision of whether or not to go after those targets, and that we can create a mind-set to go beyond fear and indecision. The question now is, how do we actually get to that target, dream, goal, or ambition? By using exactly what Karen used to eventually walk away with that $2 million: the **Four Critical Keys to Conquering Anything.** The keys are: *assess* the situation; *create* a simple plan; *take* action; and *evaluate* your progress. You can remember them through the acronym **ACTE**™.

Karen took a minute to ask herself, What am I here to accomplish? Making these men treat me as an equal, or taking their account for $2 million?

First she used a Verbal Command Request on herself to focus her energy: "Get the account." Then she assessed the situation: She couldn't undo in one business meeting these ignorant men's attitudes about women they have obviously held for their entire lives. Nor could she force them to hear her opinion directly.

In order to get through this hostile situation and come out on top, she created a simple plan: to subtly direct Peter to be the intermediate between her and the men at the meeting. If she can't guide the men, she can guide the person they are paying attention to. Then she can take action: She suggested a line of ideas for the discussion to follow, then said, "Peter probably knows more about this than I do, so I'll let Peter run with it." Whenever she wanted input from the men from the firm, she directed it as a question through Peter. Peter, meanwhile, is a smart guy who quickly picked up on the strategy, having worked with Karen for many years and being a seasoned pro in the industry.

Then, she evaluated the progress. Are the men now engaged in the process? Yes. They are asking questions, having put down their doodling and quit talking amongst themselves. They have started using phrases like, "On this first order . . ."

To survive this attack, Karen had to essentially change her role from being the head of the company to playing a support role. Is it fair? No. Did it work? Yes. She didn't have to like it, but she did it in this circumstance because it got results. On the battlefield, there's no room for ego. She did what she had to do for her company, its employees, and her future in the industry. She conquered their ignorance, walked away with the two-million-dollar contract, and bought herself a new Mercedes as a reward.

Warfare is all about strategic thinking. Strategic thinking is more than just planning, it's about gaining the greatest advantage and making the fewest mistakes. It takes into account all the many obstacles that can get in the way of you accomplishing what you want, and identifies the various factors that move you toward what you want. I developed the **Four Critical Keys to Conquering Anything** that I now use to teach self-protection from a checklist used in the military called the Four Keys to a Successful Operation. The principles, however, apply to most any situation. (See chart on p. 101.)

This thought process can be used for targets no matter what the size, no matter how complicated, how simple, how immediate, or far-reaching. Its application is universal. Once you understand the full extent of **ACTE,** it will, with practice, be available for you to use under even the most intense stress, no matter the scope or magnitude of your target.

The first element, **Assess the situation,** is like homework: The more thoroughly you complete it, the easier time you'll have when test day comes around. The better you assess, the better, and more easily, everything else will fall into place.

Assessing the situation begins with you making a choice. What are you going to tackle? I can't tell you how many people have said to me, "You're so lucky you know what you want to do in life." It's not luck—God didn't open the heavens one day and say, "Hey, Richard, do this." All I did was choose one thing that I enjoy. I enjoy doing a lot

When in Doubt, ACTE

Assess the situation: Solutions naturally evolve when you know what you are dealing with.

Create a simple plan: A simple plan is easy to remember and easy to perform and leads to a faster result.

Take action: The more direct your route in taking action, the quicker your result.

Evaluate your progress: What happened? Have my plan and my actions created my desired results? If not, start over. Assess the situation again, create a simple plan, take action. In evaluating anything, the "100 Percent Rule" should be your measuring stick: If it works 100 percent of the time, it stays. If it doesn't, fix it. If you can't fix it, get rid of it.

of different things, and I could have picked any one of them. Yet, I had to make a choice. It doesn't have to be the "perfect" thing, it just needs to be something to start your momentum, to fan the fire inside you. Choosing something always leads to something else. Choosing nothing— and choosing nothing is a choice—always leads nowhere.

If you live passively, you are forcing yourself to live reactively. One choice, no matter how small, can save you from "analysis paralysis," where you spend more time thinking about doing something than you spend actually doing it.

Once you understand what it is you are going to focus on, you have to be able to understand your target in context—what's all around it? There are a few systematic ways to assess that.

It begins with observation. People use their eyes, but they rarely see what's happening in their world. One of the exercises I do in Bukido to teach how to assess whether a person presents a physical threat or not is to ask students, What's the first thing you should look at when a person approaches you? "The eyes," they invariably say.

I walk up to them. "Right now," I tell them in a menacing voice, "I'm going to kick your butt with my eyes." And I give them the fiercest stare that I have in my repertoire.

For a split second they're taken aback, then they realize nothing is happening and nothing will happen.

"I must be losing my touch," I say, still keeping the stare. "It always works in the Mickey Spillane novels. . . ."

Then they learn the correct answer: the hands. Always look at a person's hands. The reason for that is if somebody has a knife or a gun, there is a 99.9 percent chance he or she will be carrying it in his hands. If his or her hands are empty, then I look at his approach to my "action zone," a 3-and-a-half to 4-foot imaginary circle that surrounds my body. I can see if his or her hands are reaching for something, and if so, then I pick a target. Even in a nonlethal situation the hands are important—they tell whether a person is anxious, or impatient, or smokes a lot, or is married, or works outside. You can't avoid using your hands, and as a result they give away more about our lives than we're even conscious of.

A scout/sniper is trained through a systematic

process, so that instead of looking around haphazardly he doesn't miss anything. In Bukido I teach the same concepts used in sniper training through observation drills such as this: I take a student and face him toward the wall so he can't see what's going on behind him. I then take two quarters. I place one about six feet from him off to one side or other of his centerline. The other I put right next to the heel of his foot. While I'm doing this I have him cover his ears, close his eyes, and make noises so he can't hear the quarters touch the ground. When I'm done I tell him to open his eyes and turn around.

"Two quarters are on the ground," I say. "If you can stay where you are and find them, you're fifty cents richer."

I step off to one side of him, but I watch his eyes. He starts looking every which way, all over the place, then he sees the one six feet in front of him.

"Got one," he says.

"Good, but there's one more to go."

Invariably, his eyes will dart everywhere again—he'll scan the ceiling, ask to see behind the door. He shifts his eyes all over the place, trying to see the whole room at one time with no set technique. Finally, I give him a clue by reminding him it's on the floor. Frustrated, he looks at his feet and, surprise, there's the quarter.

"Too late," I tell him. "If the quarters had been snakes, which one would have bit you? If they had been knives, which one would have stabbed you? If they had been men, which one would be more dangerous? And if they had been guns, which one wouldn't have missed?"

The message is clear and the impact immediate: The closest threat is the one you have to pick up first, not last.

It seems the human tendency is to look at everything as being "out there" without realizing that without the first, closest step, nothing goes anywhere.

Systematic observation begins by scanning from near to far, then from right to left. You have to do this like you are radar. Go in sweeping motions where you are covering yourself as you reach out to the farthest reaches of the room or your vision. Try it the next time you're looking for a woman's earring, or your keys. You'll find that in this way you can see things in a formatted order, allowing your brain to quickly register information, process it, and take action, if necessary. This is true whether you're facing a dozen armed assassins or if you're walking into the company Christmas party—from what I hear from my clients, the dynamics aren't very different. The point is, with systematic observation you develop the habit of never missing anything and of making a ruthless evaluation of what truly exists.

For me this has also been a metaphor for finding my path to a goal or dream. You must always start with the

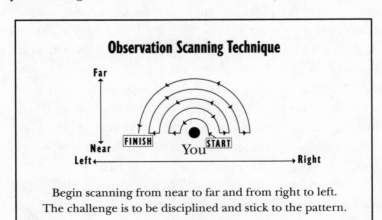

Observation Scanning Technique

Begin scanning from near to far and from right to left.
The challenge is to be disciplined and stick to the pattern.

closest thing, and that is always going to be yourself. This is the thing you can have an immediate impact on. You need to be able to assess four major factors: What do I have? What do I need? What are my strengths? What are my weaknesses? Some weaknesses can be addressed, some weaknesses can't be, and so must just be taken into account when you are ready to create your plan.

But before you get to that, there are a few more things to assess: No matter what your long-term goal is, short-term targets are in front of it. That means as you use the scanning process of observation, you must see the targets that are now in front of you. Some targets are there because the industry or government or boss says they have to be there; some we put in front of ourselves, like acquiring a new skill or developing a friendship or alliance.

Once you have completed a CARVER matrix and prioritized your targets (see chapter 1), the target that is considered most valuable becomes your *mission*. A mission is comprised of primary and secondary targets. Let's say you have selected a mission. Now you must ask yourself, What specific targets will move me closer to accomplishing my mission? Once I have answered this question and laid out a series of targets, I now have to assess which of these targets is the closest to me. Which can I have an immediate impact on? These become my primaries. Targets that are farther away from me, that are more difficult to get to right now, become the secondaries. I rarely go beyond developing a secondary list of targets because a lot can change after I knock down some primaries. I want to be flexible, and I don't want to overextend my resources while I am still in the process of assessing the value of a given group of targets.

How do you use this in an everyday situation? Let's say you're self-employed and are concerned about your finances. Through the CARVER matrix you've decided that setting up a retirement fund is the first thing you have to do to establish future financial security. A retirement fund then becomes your mission. What are some of the things you need to accomplish your mission? Money, a place to put it, and a way to go about doing it. The problem is that these things are pretty vague and don't provide clear, measurable targets. What you need to do is define a target that is right next to you that can either provide you with more information on how best to proceed, or that can move you directly toward the accomplishment of your mission.

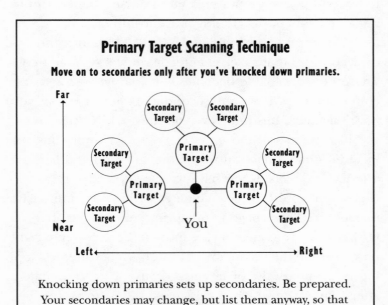

Primary Target Scanning Technique

Move on to secondaries only after you've knocked down primaries.

Knocking down primaries sets up secondaries. Be prepared. Your secondaries may change, but list them anyway, so that you're always pushing yourself toward the next target.

You know that a friend of yours has just set up an IRA (individual retirement account) and she understand the whole process. Because she is closest to you, talking to her will become your primary target. Having the money, a place to put it, and a way to go about doing it will become your secondary targets. This means that you will not focus on them until you have spoken to her. After you talk to her, you will then have some new targets to pursue. Be sure to organize these new targets in the same way: The closest or primary targets should be the first you focus on. Once they are knocked down, then move on to the secondary targets that are farther away. With each target that you knock down, you will move closer and closer to the

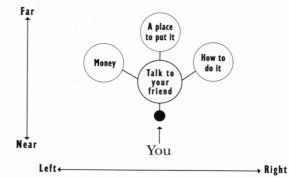

Primary Target for Retirement Account

Move on to secondaries only after you've knocked down primaries.

Stay focused on knocking down your primary target. Don't get distracted by trying to focus on too many things at once. Staying focused reduces fear and minimizes stress.

accomplishment of your mission: the setting up of a retirement account. Congratulations!

Organizing things by primaries and secondaries helps you focus on what is right in front of you, like that quarter from the observation drill. Stress and confusion come from trying to focus on too many things at one time. They lead to feeling overwhelmed, which can greatly impede or shut down your progress. When you cut down the number of things you have to concentrate on, you increase the amount of focus you can bring to knocking down a clearly defined target.

Environmental analysis is related to systematic observation. This is the point in training where my Bukido students dedicate some time to examining the environments where they work, play, and live. The goal of environmental analysis is to become really aware of what is normal and usual in their everyday life. What belongs in it? What is supposed to be here? This process was absolutely critical when I worked as an executive protection specialist— that's a fancy term for bodyguard. If I don't know what really belongs, *how will I know what doesn't?* It is what doesn't belong, no matter how small or seemingly insignificant, that is my warning indicator that a problem might exist, or even that there could be the potential for a problem to arise. For goal setting, the question is, What in my environment is going to get in the way of me knocking down my established targets?

Awareness training is the final component needed for assessing the situation. More than just observing, it is the use of all your senses to solve problems. That means: 1) kinesthetically be aware of where you are in space, how your body moves; 2) stop waiting for your turn to talk and start really listening to people. And don't just listen to the people you think you're "supposed" to listen to. Listen to everybody—you never know where your next piece of information will come from. Finally, don't forget that "the nose knows"—the olfactory sense is the one most directly linked to memory. When SEALs were "in country" in Vietnam they would eat what the enemy ate, because if they did not the very smell of them eating American food would stand out in that environment.

You will be surprised at what you can put together using all your senses in harmony. I often hear intuition talked about as if it were some kind of mystic phenomenon. I believe in intuition, in fact I rely on it, but I believe it is the result of using one if not all of your five senses—hearing, seeing, feeling, smelling, tasting—to optimum effect, together with evaluated experience of past events. The synthesis of these together, which happens so quickly it is mostly unconscious, creates the sixth sense of intuition. You can have good or bad intuition. You can misread the input gathered from using your senses, and you can make a poor evaluation of your experiences, and you'll come up with bad intuition. Good intuition results from the proper use of your senses plus careful and smart evaluation of experience. But, since intuition usually happens on such an unconscious level, the use of it is haphazard. Through rigorous awareness training, the senses are trained and intuition develops, rising to a conscious level. That's when it truly becomes a sixth sense, something that can be readily and reliably called upon.

In the media you often see intuition packaged with

fear. "Something told me there was something wrong about that guy," or "I knew something was off but I didn't do anything." They are always statements made from a hindsight perspective. They show a systematic refusal to pay attention to something that their senses brought in— not magic hocus-pocus senses, but things you see, hear, smell, and feel. Then they failed to put that together with good evaluation of the experience. Because they waited until they were in a state of fear to notice things, the tendency in most cases was to shut down and let somebody else take charge of them. Be like your cat or dog—use your senses to be in the here and now of every moment.

Another effect of awareness training is that it cultivates your curiosity. The bottom line is: Assume nothing, ask a lot of questions, and verify as much as you can.

The second part of the acronymn ACTE is to **Create a simple plan**. You can be imaginative in your planning but if it's not simple to execute, then redesign it. Or trash it. A plan should answer these three core questions—and if you do this, you'll be way ahead of most people:

The Three Core Questions of a Plan

1. How do I get there?
2. What do I do when I get there?
3. How do I get *out* of there?

Something as basic and routine as a to-do list is a plan. It's daily practice in strategic thinking. When I served as the special projects coordinator for SEAL Team Two's Intelligence Department, I realized that a to-do list was best when it mirrored the metabolic highs and lows we all experience in a day.

When you wake up you have energy, but you have not reached the zenith yet. So, you warm up with the relatively critical targets that are accessible. I start each day with a list of primaries. To build momentum I usually begin with a few that have both a relatively high priority and can easily be knocked down, like working out and banking.

As I gain strength and focus, I am ready to tackle the primaries that are the most critical, and I am also at my physical and mental peak of the day. That's when I schedule client contacts, advanced classes, and critical business meetings outside of the company. The timing usually works well because the tendency is for the most critical targets not to be immediately accessible—for instance, chances are I'm not going to be able to meet with a video producer first thing in the morning or after normal business hours. When I approach these primaries, I already have the momentum of success behind me, having knocked down the primaries I schedule daily.

I save the primaries that are the most accessible, but the least critical, for the end so that I can wrap up on a successful note when my energy and focus are starting to lose their edge. This is when I'll oversee an evening class of beginning students (less physically demanding than advanced classes), return personal phone calls, or grocery shop.

Once you have a plan, rehearse the most critical

primary targets a few times. For me, it's my business meetings and client contacts, because that is how my business grows. Doing this will prepare you for the moment you have to act. Marksmen often train using a technique called "dry firing." Essentially, what they do is make the weapon completely safe, without ammunition, then work their techniques over and over again until a firm but relaxed grip, alignment of the front to rear sights, a steady trigger pull, and a visual sharpening of their focus on the front sight of the weapon becomes as automatic as breathing. Today, I "dry fire" a meeting— going over the points I want to make, what I will say, how I want it to go.

Ultimately, your ability to create simple plans and take action is important because people don't pay you for hours that you work or for your education, per se. They pay you for the value you bring. *The better your plan, the more valuable your actions are.* It's just that simple.

After my plan is in place comes the third part: I just **Take action**. Without action, everything else you've done up to this point is useless, a series of interesting mental exercises, nothing more. In SEAL Team, when we are doing combative swimmer operations—which means we attack ships with bombs strapped to our backs—we say, "Plan your dive, then dive your plan." The theory is that you think more clearly in planning than you do under the stress of action. So the more you can act according to plan, the smoother everything runs. It's about staying focused and finishing what you know.

Finally, **Evaluate**. What worked? What didn't? What can I do the same? What could I do differently next time?

When you evaluate, you are teaching yourself how to ACT—*assess* the situation, *create* a simple plan, and *take* action. You are grading yourself, and you have to be honest. If you did a crappy job, tell yourself that, but know that you can learn from a crappy job. What you are trying to do is learn how to get it right more often, not sit around beating yourself up over what you've done wrong. Fix what can be fixed. If it can't be fixed, try something else.

In this way you'll develop your Standard Operating Procedures, or SOPs. Once you start knocking down targets, you'll recognize a pattern to the things that turn out right. This pattern can become the basis for your Standard Operating Procedure. For example, I understand that treating people with courtesy gets results. Courtesy then becomes an SOP. An SOP is a fail-safe process to get things done: Thoughts require energy. The more I condition a specific thought, the less energy it takes to bring that thought into reality. This produces faster results reliably. It's like loading a macro on your computer, where you program one key to perform the function it previously took five separate keys in a certain sequence to produce the same result. A macro saves you time so you can get to the important work, which is thinking up new ideas and acting on them.

While some targets fall down right away, others may take years. Don't stall out in the evaluation process. Take a deep breath, and start the ACTE cycle all over again. That's how you'll keep moving forward.

It sometimes seems to me that life is a series of pop quizzes. The best tests of what you know come when you least expect them. This test came when our officer received orders for us to do a security test for the marines who guarded an air force communications installation in the Philippines. It was the mid-eighties, and the NPA (New People's Army), headquartered in Manila, were making a habit of sending small bands of "sparrow units" to capture or assassinate foreign and domestic military leaders. The NPA then used the hostages to strong-arm the government and leverage their way to legitimacy. This particular communications installation was headed by an air force lieutenant colonel, just the kind of leader the local terrorist groups were looking for.

Tim, Rusty, and I were tapped for the assignment. Our job was to get into the windowless, one-story secured facility and somehow take the colonel hostage. We were supposed to press for three demands as conditions of his release: have our cause broadcast over the military satellite network, release one of our brothers in arms from the U.S. government, and secure safe passage for ourselves, which in our case would be SEAL SOP: Get back to the ocean. Once we're there, we have the advantage over almost anyone. That was all the instruction we had, the rest would be up to us. We had to act as ruthlessly and unpredictably as real terrorists in order to give the best training to the marines. This was in the early days before terrorism had grown into the deep-rooted global threat that it is today, and dealing with terrorist tactics wasn't yet standard training for most branches of the military. SEAL Team was the exception, because our unit had actually been formed to out-Vietcong the Vietcong.

The marines knew a test was coming, so once they

heard the colonel was nabbed they would know not to use live ammunition. But this wasn't a run-of-the-mill drill— they didn't know exactly what we were going to do, and they didn't know when we'd strike. The three of us only had a few hours' notice to prepare for this. It was my first such operation, but I was looking forward to working with two pros like Tim and Rusty.

First we had to assess the situation. We examined information on the surrounding area, familiarized our-selves with a blueprint of the building, and looked at maps of access roads. Our resources for the assignment were what we could carry: three weapons loaded with blanks and three backpacks with basic escape and eva-sion gear.

Then, we created a simple plan. We didn't plan very far into the operation because there were too many unknowns—our secondary targets might change once we saw where we were after our first few targets were knocked down. We did know the operation overseers assumed we were going to be holed up in the building, and the marines were acting on the assumption that they were either going to peacefully negotiate us out of the building, or storm in and "kill" us.

A few hours later, it was time to take action. We took a standard navy van from the garage pool, spray painted PWD (for Public Works Division) on the sides, and drove to the gates. Dressed in civilian coveralls with hard hats, we looked like general construction workers from the base. Tim smiled and waved at everybody and showed the guard a fake work request sheet. It was amazing how easy it was to get through simply by acting as if we had every right to be there.

We pulled around to the side of the communications building and unloaded a bin with some toolboxes. It looked as if we were going to work on an electrical problem inside the building. We'd only thrown empty toolboxes on the top of the bin, under them, the bin was filled with our backpacks and weapons.

The blueprint had told us exactly where the colonel's office suite was located, so we just blithely strolled in. Tim knocked on the colonel's door to see if he was inside.

"What is it?" the colonel snapped, irritated at the interruption.

Tim opened the door and the colonel stood up to see who would be so rude as to barge in without being announced. Rusty slipped past Tim, and before the colonel had a chance to grasp what was really going on, Rusty had a Beretta 92F-9mm pointed at his temple. I was right behind them, pushing the bin in through the door. Once in, I pushed it to one side and drew my weapon. Tim shut the door and walked to the colonel. I stayed at the door and covered the entrance.

"Please sit down, Colonel. I believe you are expecting us?" Tim said. His tone was respectful but he couldn't help but be intimidating. He was the kind of guy who could have, and had, bitten a nose or ear off an enemy stupid enough to come after him.

"Yes, I was expecting you, but I thought this was going to happen a week ago," replied the colonel, who was himself no shrinking violet. "You guys are late."

Tim shrugged, still smiling. "Well, sir, they only call us when it absolutely, positively has to be destroyed overnight."

"So how do you want to play this?" the colonel said.

"The first thing we're going to do is clear the building of everybody except you," Tim told him. "What's the best way to do this without hurting any of your people?" The idea was to proceed the way terrorists usually do. The colonel knew all this, and said the safest bet was for him just to call his second-in-charge and tell him to make everyone leave.

The colonel looked at Rusty, who still held the gun. "Does he have to point that thing at me the entire time?"

Tim nodded. "Until the building is cleared."

Within ten minutes the single-floor building was empty of all personnel. Rusty and I quickly secured all of the building's doors by locking them from the inside. Now it was down to just three SEALs and one air force colonel. Back in the colonel's office, we shed our PWD coveralls and put on our camouflage. With the cammies on we could slip out and melt into the surrounding jungle, if— or when—we had to.

We turned on the TV in the office to watch the satellite broadcast to see what, if anything, the military news was reporting about our surprise visit to the installation. Nothing yet. I turned down the volume. We'd no doubt be receiving a call from the security chief soon, but in the meanwhile Tim and Rusty doubled-checked our gear while I took out some neoprene rubber, tape, and fake blood we'd brought along to underline the realism of the situation. I got busy making a couple of fake bloody "fingers," just in case the marines needed a reminder of how dangerous and serious a terrorist situation would be.

The phone finally rang. The captain of security for

the marine task force was on the line. Tim handed me the list of demands.

"You should record this, Captain," I told him, and proceeded to read the three items we required. Each had to be met within a three-hour deadline. "Call back in fifteen minutes and report to us what you've done" was the only thing I said as I hung up the phone.

The three of us had until that phone call to assess what kind of a situation we had in front of us. Since we were not being monitored, and we had no way to get any more information than what we'd come in with, we had to keep our plan as simple as possible.

Fifteen minutes later, the phone rang.

"We haven't been on TV," I said. "Have our brothers in arms been released?" I asked. Tim looked at me questioningly. I shook my head to tell him, no, none of the demands had been met.

"Do it," he said. We hadn't practiced this, but I knew what he meant. We hadn't prepared those fake fingers just to pass the time.

I said over the receiver, "Because of you the colonel has now lost a finger. If we don't hear from you in five minutes, he loses another one." And I hung up. We had now accelerated the pace.

There were only two doors from which the marine strike force could enter the building, the side and the front, both of which we locked from the inside. I hustled to get to the side door. Quickly but quietly I cracked the door, in time to see the back of a marine's head. He was first in front of a long line of troops ready to storm the door, but unfortunately, he was checking in back of him rather than watching the door. He turned back with a shocked look as I pitched a bloody rubber finger into his face. The rest of the marines backed up for a split second, just long enough for me to slam the door and lock it again. I could hear them forcing the door as I hurried back into the office where Tim and Rusty waited with the colonel.

"They're ready to enter," I said. "If that door doesn't give in the next second or two, they'll be moving around to the other one, if they're not already there."

"I guess we'll get to see what it looks like when marines storm in," the colonel said, settling back into his chair.

Tim turned to look at him and said, "Do you seriously think I am going to let them kill me?"

The colonel looked confused. "But that's the exercise."

"That's your exercise, sir, not mine," Tim told him. I could see Tim was thinking about what we might possibly be able to do next. All of this was happening more quickly than we'd imagined.

"I know exactly how we can get out of here," Rusty said as he came back in from making a final sweep around the offices. "You're going to love this. Come with me."

We took the colonel and followed Rusty down a hall and through a side door, which took us straight into a garage bay located in the back of the building. Not only that, two new camouflage-painted trucks sat there, calling our names. Rusty jingled a set of keys he found hanging obviously on a hook. "Ta da!"

"Holy Mary," I said, "I love this job." The competitive juices were flowing now—the marines wanted to get us, but we didn't want to be got.

We loaded our packs into the back of the pickup and
Rusty hopped in to keep everything from rolling around.
Tim took the driver's seat, and I put the colonel in the
middle of the passenger's seat. I slid in with my Beretta
drawn.

"Sorry about the finger," I joked with the colonel.

Rusty pulled the bay door open and got in the back
as we pulled away. We quickly drove toward the front
entrance of the installation only to find a marine vehicle
at the gate, but the way it was parked gave us enough
room to get by. However, the bigger problem was the
marine standing in the middle of the road with his M16
drawn at us.

Tim gunned the truck and headed right toward him.
I don't even think his blood pressure increased, he looked
as if he was just driving the kids to Sunday school. The
marine realized just in the nick of time that Tim wasn't
about to stop. He jumped out of the way, rolling in the dirt
as we passed.

The base was huge. We were headed out on a long
road that would eventually take us off the base, if we could
get that far. This was a straight stretch of road that seemed
to reach all the way to the horizon. The colonel started to
look a little nervous—obviously nothing was going as he
had anticipated.

"How are you doing?" I asked.

"It's been a long time since I've been able to play out
of the office like this," he said with a tight smile. The look
on his face seemed to be saying that he had taken for
granted the fact that the security force would save him, and
now they weren't acting as he had assumed they would.

As we raced from the base compound, we could see

vehicles off in the distance approaching us at high speeds. Tim's eyes scanned the terrain with near mechanical precision. He saw exactly what he was looking for, and floored the pickup. When he slammed the brakes, we jerked forward, and it took a second for me to realize we were on a narrow bridge that covered a small river. Tim looked to the right and we saw the blue ocean on the horizon.

When we pulled up to a stop, Tim said, "Let's go." Tim stepped out of the vehicle while Rusty gathered our gear for our return to the water. He looked back almost absentmindedly. "It was a pleasure, Colonel. Good-bye."

Then Tim looked at me and nodded. I knew what that signal meant. I looked at the colonel, pointed the gun at his head, and said, "Bye." For a second the colonel looked truly scared. Was I actually going to pull the trigger?

I said, "Bang!" Then I, too, stepped out of the vehicle, and pointed my gun in the air, shooting off a blank. This was to tell the marines that they were too late. If this had been a real terrorist attack, the colonel would already be dead.

But the game wasn't over. We now had to make it to the ocean. We started heading into the bush. When I took one last look back I could see two marine vehicles pulling up to the truck where the colonel waited. Tim saw it, too; we needed to create a new plan. He gave the hand signal for us to form a hasty ambush. We headed into the stream and sucked back into the mud of the stream banks, becoming one with the ground. We heard the marines trampling through the surrounding foliage, searching for us. There's nothing quite like the sound of a dozen or so marines who are really pissed off.

They formed a line shoulder to shoulder about ten

feet apart, moving across a wide-open field like men searching for an avalanche victim. Finally they moved past us, and Tim gave us a hand signal to melt into the stream. As the current from the stream took us out to sea, the voices of the young marines yelling at one another rose over the sound of the water. Desperately they were trying to find those damn SEALs. It stuck in my mind, underlining a point that would be reinforced again and again during my career: It's difficult to come back and win when you start from a reactive position, like those unfortunate marines.

When the salt water hit us a few minutes later, that was the end of the game. We'd made it out to sea. On the beach to meet us were our SEAL controller, the captain of the marine security force, and the air force master sergeant who had overseen the operation. Everybody was quiet. Finally the air force sergeant stepped up. "That was pretty informative," he said. "Pretty informative indeed."

We drove to the debriefing site; now it was time to evaluate. When we pulled up to the security building, all the marines and air force personnel involved with the exercise were standing out front. They had looks of surprise and amazement on their faces. They were astonished, as if some kind of miraculous event had taken place. Yet, all we had done was set up targets and knocked them down, one right after the other. If we had not known how to ACTE, the whole operation could have quickly become mired in confusion. But we did know how to implement strategic thinking, so for us what could have been an incredibly complicated operation became a simple series of processes: Assessing the situations, Creating simple plans, Taking action, and Evaluating the results.

Chapter 5

Master Your Weapons

The more I sweat in peace, the less I bleed in war.
—*SEAL Commandment*

Trust me on this: A weapon that jams in the heat of combat doesn't do you any good—and will most likely get you killed. Skills are your own private arsenal of weapons you deploy to hit your target. The better your weapons, the easier it is to hit your targets. The more skills you have, the more flexible you are, and it's that flexibility that will ensure your victory.

In Bukido training, once I have introduced you to the concept of targets, we talk about the weapons that best match those targets. We make sure that the weapons we use always damage the chosen target, not ourselves. Then we talk about the movement associated with those weapons. Students never use any weapon that is beyond their current skill level, because I don't want them to be preoccupied in the thick of battle with guessing which weapon is best. I want them to *know*. In the military they say, "Master one weapon, don't try to master all of them." The reason for this is that once you have mastered one, then all weapons relate to the one you have mastered.

In the beginning, students are limited in their weapon choice. But as time goes by and they master the weapons they have available, they find they are very flexible with those weapons.

The following chart provides my beginning students with a checklist of basic weapons immediately at their disposal.

Beginning Students' Weapons

Targets	Weapons
Eyes and Throat	Fingertips
Nose, Eardrums, and Groin	Palms
Groin, Nose, Throat, and Joints	Knees
Groin, Nose, and Throat	Shins
Head and Joints	Heel Stomp

Although this is designed for use in hand-to-hand combat, the idea is that no matter what you're tackling, only give yourself a few things at the beginning to work on to avoid being overwhelmed. One of my students, Dana, just landed her first teaching job out of college and reports that she used the chart from Bukido to organize her class. Here's one of her many versions of the chart:

Targets	Weapons
Maximize class time	Lesson plans: Build around primaries, secondaries
Improve retention of reading assignments	Homework: One page oral report, memorize one short poem a week
Increase computer literacy	Computer lab: computer company employee volunteered to do class visit
Engage parents in students' learning	Open house; calls home; class assignment to write story of an ancestor

The goal is really to go beyond thinking about the weapon and solely focus on the target. The target's position determines which weapon will be used, and how the weapon will be used. You work and train a weapon to such a degree it simply becomes an extension of your body. It is as much a part of you as are your fingers, eyes, lips, and tongue. The weapons require as little thought to perform their function as blinking. If I can operate five different things that don't require a lot of energy, I can get a tremendous amount done. Think again about the example of the light switch: You don't have to think about your finger when you turn on a light switch. You barely think about the light switch itself.

I learned this concept in association with the use of weapons like the M60 machine gun, the McMillan 86 sniper rifle with a Leupold 10x scope, and a Tanto full-tang Cold-Steel knife—because, let's face it, during the occasions you need to use those, you don't have time to think, Gee, how does this thing work? The principle, however, applies to the use of any skill or ability. I have a student who majored in French and lived in France, and as a result she speaks the language like a native. I studied French in the Special Forces Language School, but I just know the rudiments of the language. I asked her what it was like to speak fluently. She shrugged, "I don't think about it. If the person in front of me speaks French, that's what I use to get my point across." Her ability is her weapon, and the target is communication.

Once you have walked through the paper-thin mist of fear, you have to have something to do on the other side. The answer to what you have to do is deploy your weapon. Without this task to focus on, the fear will return twice as strong. This is where training plays such a critical part in your performance. The way you train dictates the quality of your chosen action, how easy it will be for you to use your weapon, and thus how efficiently you knock down your target.

How you practice determines the quality of your performance in deploying a weapon. *Perfect performances can't exist without perfect practice.* The **Training Pyramid** is a systematic method that allows the progression of learning to occur naturally. This provides a way to acquire more weapons (i.e., skills) you don't already possess.

My experiences in training for close-quarter battle honed my thinking about training in general, and introduced me to the ideas behind the Training Pyramid. Close-quarter battle essentially means clearing and securing rooms from terrorists who have taken hostages. In other words, we get rid of the bad guys. This is the most volatile situation imaginable: You have merely a fraction of a second to determine who are the "tangos" (terrorists) and who are the hostages. Not only that, it's highly possible to shoot one of your own people, because a full-fledged battle will be raging in a space that might be the size of a bedroom. Bullets travel through plasterboard and wood, and if the room is made from concrete or steel there is the danger of ricochet. It's not uncommon for explosives to go off before and during your entrance.

How do we prepare to face this absolute chaos? Reduce the entire process down into distinct increments, second by second. Then, after everyone knows exactly where he is supposed to be, what he is supposed to do, and how he is supposed to move, all the pieces are slowly and gradually put back together. It is a dangerous piece of choreography. People have been shot and killed just in the training.

The Training Pyramid ensures that in every step along the way skills are learned correctly and thoroughly developed, so you have them when you need them most.

Before I go further in the discussion of the Training Pyramid, I want to give you a quick example of it: typing.

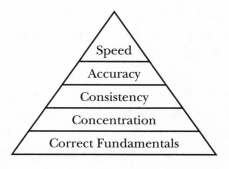

The process of learning to type—or not learning to type!—is exactly what I'm talking about. First you have to familiarize yourself with the keyboard, exactly where all the letters, numbers, and symbols are placed. Then you have to learn how to position your hands so that you can strike the basic keys you need to learn first. These are examples of the *correct fundamentals.* Next you have to *concentrate* to be able to physically move your fingers over the keyboard in a way that will produce legible words. To concentrate fully in the beginning, you need to fully, slowly focus on the fundamentals you were given. You repeat those concentrated movements over and over again to be able to be *consistent,* hitting the keys you want to hit, getting the same correct results over and over again. Assuming that you have applied the correct fundamentals, concentration, and consistency, you will find that you are over time able to make fewer and fewer typos and look at the keyboard less and less. Now you are developing *accuracy.* Finally, as your typing gets more accurate until it feels like second nature, your speed will gradually and naturally increase. Over time you will find you are able to type as fast as you talk! But if something breaks down in the process—you don't learn correct fundamentals, or you don't concentrate on what you learn, or you don't have the patience to practice often enough to develop consistency—you'll end up like me. A rotten typist.

Correct fundamentals are the basics, the foundation on which everything rests. Every new skill has basics to it. Coaches talk about "being in the zone," or "flow," or just "peak performance." It feels the same, no matter what you're doing: There's a sense that you are controlling everything, a feeling of timelessness where action happens in slow motion, being hypersensitive to everything you are physically experiencing, and a belief that anything might be possible. But without correct fundamentals, achieving this state is impossible. If the fundamentals are learned incorrectly, performance will be inconsistent. Results will be slipshod at best. If you think you know what you're doing but perform inconsistently, the more you'll be frustrated at your uneven performance. Sometimes this is why a beginner can beat an expert, because if the beginner only knows a little information but knows it correctly, he can focus on that to get results. Meanwhile the expert gets frustrated because he keeps telling himself, This shouldn't be happening. The expert tends to make things more complicated.

My brother, John, is no Bjorn Borg, but he is a much better tennis player than I am. But when we play tennis, he tends to try the more difficult techniques, like slicing the ball to create top or bottom spin so that when the ball hits the ground or my racket, it jumps in an unexpected direction. Luckily for me, he is not an expert at this advanced stuff. He spends a lot of focus and energy trying to beat me using techniques that are fancy. I just concentrate on hitting the ball in a direction where he has to run to get it, or I hit it directly at him to force him to square up and volley the ball back to me. This basic technique can work for me for a complete game, or set, or maybe even a match. So sometimes I get to walk home the winner, but when he focuses on what he does best he wins. Because he has a better grasp of the fundamentals, when he leaves the fancy stuff alone and just sticks to those fundamentals he knows better than me, he beats me like a dirty rug. That's why he wins most of the time.

Concentration comes after the fundamentals have been clearly and completely defined. To fully sharpen your concentration you need four things to work in harmony. The first is *attention,* the second *alertness,* the third *focus,* and the last *control.* This maximizes the energy you have to use to accomplish the given objective. The reason soldiers are called to attention in the military is so that they are physically placed into a state of alertness, ready to receive their next order. Now the group is completely alert to the possibilities involved in whatever they're doing. Once they receive the order, they now have something to completely focus on. That is the reason a general can have control on the battlefield, because every soldier is focused completely on his task. But in this war, you're both the soldier and the general.

You know you've achieved true concentration when everything but the correct fundamentals feels outside and away from your body. You and the thing you are doing are the only things that exist on the planet.

In sniper training, they gave us a visualization tool that allowed us to develop laserlike concentration, called a sniper bubble. Let me backtrack for a moment here and reiterate that being a sniper means you're not some yahoo on top of a building taking potshots at innocent bystanders. You are a military instrument of surgical precision. You have to grasp a thousand factors that play into one shot, because there is no second shot. A sniper must take into consideration the wind variance, thermal activity—the way heat plays off the earth—distance, how the target is moving, the grain of a bullet, how fast his own heart is beating. You cannot spare one one-hundredth of a second on the fight last night

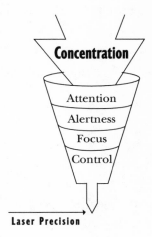

with your girlfriend, or how hungry you are, or where you need to be next. You visualize a bubble around you that seals you off from the rest of the world, and the only things that matter are the things that happen within that bubble.

It feels like there is a gradual shutting off of the outside world, a void opens up separating me from everything else. It creates two worlds: mine and the outside. In one the normal activity of everyday life continues. In the other, only me, my rifle, my target, and my training remain. Then my world condenses, it comes in *toward* me. Everything in my world intensifies. Whatever is connected to this rifle is the only thing that exists—there are no bugs or sun or rain or mud.

Sniper school is an intense course that runs seven days a week for nearly three months. It is a coveted school because it represents the ultimate in precision. To be a sniper means you are someone who reaches for a higher standard, someone with superior field craft skills, a true professional even among the SEALs. When I was there, I had two things working against me—one was a chief who didn't want to lose a man in the middle of a demanding workup for his platoon. The other was that I wore glasses, so I wasn't considered a likely candidate to make a good sniper. But because I had done a decent job on all of my assignments, my lieutenant and chief felt they needed to pay attention to my request. Once accepted into the school, I had to perform at the course's extremely high standard throughout the entire training, otherwise it was back to the platoon. Because they took a chance on the blind kid, if I failed, that cloud would stay with me for the rest of my SEAL career.

But regardless of how hard you worked during the course or how much you wanted to be a sniper, to graduate it all came down to one single shot. My graduation rested on completing this operational exercise: Shoot a man who trains terrorists. According to the training brief, this was the only time we had ever been able to nail down his schedule. The brief also said that, if I miss this guy, it will spark a major-scale international incident. The target, I was told, wears body armor, so I had to be ready to make a head shot on a moving target at dusk.

I related all this during my assignment's mission briefing to a room full of people.

"Let me get this straight. You're guaranteeing a head shot on a moving target at three hundred and fifty yards? There's no way you'll make that shot. You'll go to the body," the warrant officer told me with a challenging smile on his face.

"No sir," I said. "I can't. He's wearing body armor."

"We'll see," the warrant officer said, skeptically.

On test day, my sniper buddy and I traveled ten miles to get to the underground bunker area where the target was. We had to stalk in slowly to our position, I had to make the shot right at dusk, sneak out of there, then rendezvous with the helicopter that would take us back to base camp. During the entire exercise, there would be instructors posing as the enemy out there in jeeps and on foot searching for us.

Finally, we arrived at the position. I leaned into my rifle. There was nothing but my brain, my eye, the rifle, and the finger that would follow through on the trigger. Only bone supported my body in this position, no muscle was used.

We got a two-minute warning. No problem, I thought. I pointed the crosshairs on the target. He was standing, giving orders. I closed my eyes. If my natural point of aim is right, when I open my eyes my *focus* should still be on him.

I open them, and there he is. Piece of cake, I thought cockily.

That's when it happens. The bipod holding the rifle in place ripped out of the fiberglass stock of my weapon because of the combined weight of the rifle and the pressure of me leaning on it. Damn. There went my sniper bubble. What was I going to do? After all the things I had to do to get to sniper training, I could blow it because of *this?*

I felt a tinge of panic. Then that switch in my head flipped on: What's the first step to fix this? I asked myself. I brought myself to *attention.*

In my bag I had a so-called "field expedient bipod," an incredibly high-speed piece of gear—three sticks whittled down to points on the bottom end and held together at the top with rope and rubber bands. Because a McMillan 86 sniper rifle has a free-floating barrel—meaning nothing can touch the barrel because anything could alter the shot—I couldn't just tie my contraption to the barrel. To do that would throw off all the instrumentation and precision of the weapon. So, I quickly rigged the bipod in a way that made it lock into position with rubber bands behind the barrel.

By the time I finished that, I had less than forty seconds to make the shot. I took my position again.

The bipod shifted again.

I repositioned it, took my place, and it seemed to hold.

Twenty seconds.

I reacquired my target with my scope, but my heart was racing out of control. Because the first shot had to count, all the anxiety I felt was related to the unknown. Could I make that first shot? I decided I would go through the entire process of pulling off the shot, except I wouldn't put a round in the chamber. I dry fired the weapon, repeating the process seven times.

I had just five seconds before the order to "go" would come. But I felt different now. The world had been shut out. In my mind I wasn't doing the shot for the first time, I was just firing the weapon like I had been doing. It wasn't a fresh shot, just one precision shot in a series of precision shots I had already made.

My buddy said, "Zero." I loaded the weapon slowly,

methodically. I rested in my natural point of aim. No wind. All I had to do was put the scope on the target. I could see the beat of my heart slightly raising the rifle's scope at even intervals. My breathing was smooth, slow, and deep. The only thing that was needed to set the whole chain in motion was a voice that would suddenly appear like a breeze, saying, "Go!" Myself, the weapon, and the target were all one.

Then I heard it. "Go!"

The terrorist moved from the truck to the bunker, and then stood for a moment to watch the others unloading the weapons. The second he stopped, I aimed for his nose. I took a breath, exhaled half of it out, then followed through with the trigger. The weapon surprised me when it went off. I caught a glimpse of his *guthra*, the traditional Arab headdress, flying up.

Then my weapon fell off the improvised bipod, hitting the ground. I "called the shot" to my sniper buddy, telling him exactly where I thought the shot landed on the moving dummy that was my terrorist. "A half minute left," I said, which meant a half inch left from the tip of his nose.

Back at base camp, everyone who had been in the mission briefing came over to shake my hand. The warrant officer who had doubted the possibility of my getting the shot came up.

"I was impressed," he said, extending his hand. "Even some guys on my team might not have made that shot."

I said thank you, but I was thinking about the truly awesome intensity of concentration each of us has available to bring to bear when we shut out the outside world. It was this situation that led me to formulate the third statement from *Bukido's Code of the Warrior Spirit*: I will develop the ability to remain calm and composed, for even in the worst situations I will find opportunity.

Consistency is the by-product of using correct fundamentals and concentration over time. It works out like an equation: Correct fundamentals + Concentration = Consistency. It is about working toward getting something right every time you do it, because when you do it right once, you know it's possible for that to be the rule rather than the exception.

Accuracy means that you not only do it right every time, but you hit the bull's-eye. Accuracy cannot be argued with or denied. "Well done is quickly done," said Augustus Caesar, meaning that if you do it right the first time you don't waste time having to come back and fix it. I ask students, Which is more important, speed or accuracy? A large percentage think speed is more important because that's what we hear all the time—"Get rich quick," "Lose weight now," "Find answers fast." People are often beat by speed, or at least it appears that way. So, I give a little demonstration: I stand a student in front of me. I strike a menacing pose, and flick my fingers at their eyes so quickly they hardly have time to blink. It never fails to startle them. Then I say, "Was that pretty fast?"

"Yeah, I could barely see it," is the usual reply.

"Okay," I say, and as I do I smoothly, almost casually, reach up and stick my finger in their eye. It's not done quickly, but I use mechanics to take advantage of their natural blind spot—you can't see anything coming underneath your chin unless you are looking straight down. The result is, I always hit the target. My body was completely relaxed and they were not startled at all. At least not until my finger arrived in their eye. They rub their eye while I ask them again, "What's more important, speed or accuracy?" Everyone then revises their answer: "Accuracy."

In a shooting school taught by championship marksman John Shaw, he would always remind us of a principle crucial to a good shooter. He said, "Slow is fast." The importance of this concept is that it reminds you that smooth, deliberate movement is more successful than fast, jerky movement. It sets you up to understand that while speed impresses, accuracy kills—whether it's in combat, or in the courtroom, or on the court.

Speed must always be tempered by accuracy. It doesn't matter how fast Michael Jordan is, if he doesn't make the basket, it doesn't matter. If you focus on accuracy, over time speed develops as a consequence. Accuracy is a focused progression—meaning you have to consciously have it in your mind that you want to be accurate; speed, on the other hand, is a natural progression. You can only go as fast as you can be accurate.

Sprinter Michael Johnson, who won two gold medals at the Atlanta Summer Games of the Olympics, is probably one of the fastest men to ever grace the planet. But Johnson's coaches don't yell, "Run faster! Run faster!" They break down and perfect every single stride, every single movement for ultimate economy of motion. Not a fingertip is out of place. Every stride must look like every other stride. For speed to really happen, you must be relaxed. The better your skill or knowledge, the easier it will be to relax.

A beginner has a tendency to want to "get it over with," to rush through things. But true speed comes when you least expect it, when you are focused on other things.

When I teach the correct fundamentals in training, I actually make people move in slow motion. I do this primarily for two reasons. The first is control. It forces the students to focus and develop the correct muscle memory and sense where their bodies are in time and space. The second is because in a threatening situation the world does seem to move like a slow-motion picture with the sound turned down. The reason for that is the body's biochemical flight-or-fight responses are activated—endorphins pump through your system, your blood thickens, your heart and lungs speed up, even your eyesight becomes keener. When I have been faced with intense situations—imagine five guys surrounding you with your demise being the only thing on their minds—I "drop into gear." What I do mentally is put the real world above me, and I drop below that real world into a primal state. I am in "multiple attacker mode." I am not thinking. I am just letting the training do its work. It is beyond the static noise of everyday life, moving into a place where the world seems to disappear. I work systematically, one target at a time, one attacker at a time. If I destroy an arm, it's only to get to a throat. If I am taken to the ground I remove the attacker's eye or crack his larynx so that I can get to his eyes. If I see the attacker's neck open I break it. I do whatever I have to do to get to the next attacker effectively and efficiently. To be in this place, nothing must be wasted, you can't overextend yourself by spending too much time on any one thing. You can't afford to think you are overwhelmed, because if you do you *are* overwhelmed. And when that happens, you're dead. Literally.

You often hear the expression "giving it your all" or "giving 110 percent effort." I don't believe in thinking that way, or training that way. You can't put 110 percent into anything because it's against the very laws of physics. You only have 100 percent, and I believe that the closer you push yourself to 100 percent, the closer you are to shutting your body down. You can run your car at top speed for a few seconds, but after that it starts to shake, and ultimately it falls apart.

The more effective way to think is to aim for bringing all your skills to 80 percent of your maximum, in whatever you do. At this point you are able to think, to use your body to stay in balance and harmony, to flow rather than force. In sports performance, researchers call this the "steady state," because your body's systems are running at an efficient level: Lactic acid production has leveled off, the liver and kidneys have gotten rid of waste products, and oxygen delivery equals the metabolic demand for it. Hormones and other brain chemicals get released to erase sensations of pain and fatigue. To master your weapons means that you have the ability to act without having to think or reason. *You just know.*

In a perfect world, you would have a great instructor to lead you through the process of the Training Pyramid. As a SEAL, I was fortunate to have worked for a government that could afford to comb the earth for the best knowledge and make it available to me, but rarely are we in situations like that. Most of the time you have to be the one to teach yourself, whether it's on the job or learning a sport or trying to

figure out how to build an addition onto your garage.
These are some of the things I found that I have to remind
myself of as I go through this imperfect real world, always
trying to acquire new weapons to add to my arsenal of skills.

✦ Look for ways to learn the basics.

Don't try to pick up an advanced book on any subject
and expect to get it. Approach learning like a child learns
to run. Expect to crawl for a little while, then to walk for a
while. With time and patience you'll be running before
you know it.

- Look for material that simply explains the basics and how
  they are executed.
- Break down what you are trying to learn into small, simple-
  to-understand, bite-size chunks. Don't try to learn it all at
  once; remember learning is something that requires a
  journey.
- Make sure that the information you have allows you to get
  the same measurable results over and over when you try it
  out.
- By learning the basics right, you are laying a foundation
  on which you will build all of your skills.

✦ Never forget that you are a beginner, or, if you have experience, that you may have developed your abilities on an unstable foundation.

Beginners get easily frustrated and discouraged
because new skills or information can leave them feeling
foolish and/or uncoordinated. Beginners always have one

advantage in learning a completely new skill: they don't have to overcome bad habits. People with experience can easily become frustrated and discouraged because they are constantly fighting against old habits and their previous haphazard success. To them, change is uncomfortable. The older you get, the harder it is to pick up new skills and the less patience you have while trying to learn them. So many things get in the way of our learning. Sometimes it is past fears, bad habits, or just negative verbal-influence conditioning.

There's a well-known story about Bruce Lee once telling a student with a lot of training and experience that he would have to unlearn everything he had learned and start over again. This caught the student by surprise, because the student had worked long and hard with many masters to develop his skills. Bruce Lee then told the student the story of a Japanese Zen master who had a university professor come to him to learn the way of Zen. The master could see that the professor was already full of his own knowledge and wanted to impress the master with it. While the master patiently listened to the professor demonstrate his knowledge, the master began pouring the professor a cup of tea. The master filled the cup but kept pouring anyway. The professor stopped talking and watched the Zen master while the tea poured across the table.

The professor asked, "Why do you continue to pour the tea? The cup is full. It can't hold anymore."

"Like this cup," the master said, "you are full of your own opinions and speculations. How can I show you Zen unless you first empty your cup?"

The point Bruce Lee was trying to make is that you have to let go of all your old habits and preconceived notions in order to be open to learning. Anything can be learned at any stage of life, if you are patient and persistent enough to see the process to the end.

✦ **Know what type of learner you are.**

This is not about your IQ. The question is, how do you best respond to new information when it is presented to you, and how do you most easily take that information on board? Each of us responds to one of three general types of learning modes:

> **Visual learners:** They need to watch demonstrations. They need to see in order to understand.
>
> **Auditory learners:** They want to hear detailed explanation. They want to understand every piece of the process.
>
> **Kinesthetic learners:** They want to do it over and over. They usually want to work it out themselves. They need to learn by feeling it.

We are all, to some degree, a combination of these three types. One type, however, tends to be the best and most comfortable way we take in the majority of our learning. When a person is confused he often provides the best clues to what type of a learner he is. As an instructor I listen for the way he structures his questions. A visual learner will say things like, "I can't *see* how to do it. I'm having a problem *seeing* it." An auditory learner might say, "What you're *saying* to me just doesn't make sense. Maybe I'm *hearing* it wrong." A kinesthetic learner will say, "I can't *feel* this. My *body* doesn't know what it's doing." When designing a program to teach yourself anything, try to include visual, auditory, and kinesthetic drills to cover your bases and increase your chances of grasping the new skill.

✦ **Relish your victories.**

If you were learning from a good instructor, that person would constantly encourage success by getting you to completely refocus before having you demonstrate a particular skill again. This minimizes failure on the next attempt, constantly builds a momentum of success, and programs neurological memory, reducing failure and frustration. You have to do this for yourself: After a successful attempt at a new skill, relive the success by going over each thing you did right. Before you attempt to try your new skill again, take a moment to completely refocus yourself. This way you will have a much better chance of repeating your success. Remember, if you can do it once, you can do it again.

✦ **Ask a lot of questions along the way. Questions are the key to knowledge and understanding.**

This may be a cliché, it's also the truth: There is no such thing as a stupid question. Acquiring a skill is a lot more important than the fear of looking stupid. If the material that you are learning does not come with a list of questions for you to test yourself, then develop your own. This may sound foolish, but by testing yourself you will quickly find out if you really understand the material or are just going through the motions. Just by developing questions you are learning the material more thoroughly and developing better retention.

By the way, these elements are also what you should look for in a great instructor. So if you're shelling out money to learn something from someone, a personal trainer, say, or a weekend business seminar, evaluate how well the instructor is doing by using this as the gold standard.

What are we ultimately talking about with all this? Power in all that we do. Keep this in mind:

> **Pow•er:** (pou'er), *n.* 1. the ability to do or act; the capability of doing or accomplishing something.
>
> (*The Random House Dictionary of the English Language*)

Power is not about how strong you are or how fast you can move. Speed and strength are assets, but they are not requirements. It is about developing and maximizing the power potential that is available within each of us. It is about bringing only the power that is necessary to knock down the chosen target. The scholastic logician of the fourteenth century, William of Occam, said it best: "It is vain to do with more what can be done with fewer."

Once you have honed your weapons and gathered your abilities, you are ready to refine your movement. There are six factors that you have to consider if you want to move your weapons in a powerful manner, using only what is necessary to knock down a given target.

First you must have a *purpose.* Your purpose is the target you have in mind. You have to have a reason to move your weapon, otherwise it's just movement for the sake of movement.

Next, there is *attention.* As I've noted, in the military they call us to attention so that we can be brought to full alertness. Your mind and body are now prepped for action. If you aren't fully alert, you could move your weapon in a way that will hurt you or someone else. You may be a professionally trained stunt driver, but if you get behind the wheel and you are not paying attention, that may be the last time you get behind the wheel, or you could wreak havoc in your environment.

Balance is another factor. Moving a weapon with balance means you can think more clearly by providing a view of the big picture. You do not give more weight to one area over another. In this way you move in equilibrium.

After balance comes *flexibility.* Balance leads to control, control leads to flexibility. Flexibility is the ability to go from one point to another in the blink of an eye. Never be permanently set or locked in your thinking. A flexible mind is always ready to seize opportunities, and drop one ineffective weapon for another of greater use.

You won't get far without *persistence:* This comes from an undying belief in your own ability to eventually figure something out, to get something done. It is the knowing that you can get to the end.

Finally, there is *patience:* This is the ability to stay relaxed and know that, eventually, something will open up and then you will seize that moment.

A warrior develops from the mind out to the body; out from the body, to tools or skills just beyond his body, and from there out to the world itself. The warrior knows his mind is his ultimate weapon. The more he sharpens it, the more he can cut through the B.S.

In SEAL Team, there is never a time when we are not training. You should constantly be in training for something, because you can never know anything too well on which your life depends. That's the idea behind the Training Pyramid—if you know how to start from a foundation and build up, you can learn anything in a way that will produce reliable skills.

As you develop the warrior within you, you come to understand that the pursuit of that ideal is what life is all about. It's why you exist on this planet. The warrior never underestimates the value of training, because he/she never underestimates the challenges that will face him/her.

Chapter 6

Guarantee the Win

The ideal general wins the war before the battle is
ever fought.

—*Sun Tzu*

Sometimes it feels like I never left the teams, because it
seems I hear the term "Navy SEALs" every day. It feels
like everybody and their brother says they were a SEAL, or
they are selling a training system that "trained the Navy
SEALs." Good for them—the SEALs do comb the earth
for the best training available, taking a little bit from that
system, a little bit from this, because you never know
where you're going to pick up the most useful information. But why does the association with Navy SEALs mean
so much and have such marketing power? Because the
name is synonymous with winning.

What most people don't understand, though, is that
we don't win because we're a tough bunch of badasses—
we're a tough bunch of badasses because we do our homework and refuse to quit. We don't train to fight, we train

to *win*. We have a saying, "It's easy to be hard, but it's hard to be smart." Now I'm going to tell you everything I believe is contained within that little axiom:

Sometimes opportunity comes to you, but most of the time you have to move toward it. A SEAL never relies on luck or chance, because he knows that both can just as easily go in his opponent's favor. The truth is that the best "luck" often follows the hardest work. Gather your abilities, then prepare to make opportunities for yourself.

A SEAL has been taught to understand that there are consequences for every action. This is why he weighs his actions, so that he knows in advance whether the battle is worth the fight it will take to win it.

The **Advantage-Stacking Thought Process** will help you do this. *Advantage stacking* is another strategic planning tool to organize many of the ideas we've talked about in the previous chapters. You want to stack so many of the advantages in your favor that, when the order comes, when the opportunity presents itself, you can't help but win. Every successful person, whether they realize it or not, stacks advantages. We never used this term in the teams, but this was what we were doing every minute of the day.

Advantage stacking, put together with the Action Mind-set, builds an intensity of commitment to everything you do. It underlies the effectiveness and efficiency of every given action you choose to take. It's about clearly demonstrating that you are able to defeat the enemy before the first battle is ever fought. If you demonstrate complete superiority and absolute commitment to eliminating the threat of the enemy, a smart enemy will see that to wage war with you is complete folly. The enemy that is blind or ignorant, however, will still attempt to wage war with you. Let me give you an example: In executive protection, the bodyguard does not try to create a situation in which the person being protected is invulnerable. That would be a waste of time and effort, because complete safety is impossible. Everyone is vulnerable, to some degree. But a smart bodyguard will stack every possible advantage in his favor to make his "protectee," or "principal," so difficult a target that he or she is not worth the effort and the potential consequence the bad guy would have to suffer in order to succeed. This is called "hardening the target."

Advantage stacking is one more element that gives you the courage and confidence to act because it promotes efficient and decisive action. Advantage stacking as a mind-set costs very little in effort, resources, and time when compared to the benefits that you will reap when you act successfully.

Advantage stacking really comes down to answering questions that make the difference between success and failure. I created the acronym **ADVANTAGES** as an easy checklist of questions that must be answered well in advance of the moment you need to act:

A **Attitude**

D **Desire**

V **Visualization**

A **Attention**

N **Necessity**

T **Timing**

A **Alliances**

G **Gear**

E **Emergency**

S **Skills**

The more advantages you stack in your favor, the more you show yourself and everyone else how badly you want to knock down the target. Let's go down the list:

A: *Attitude.* Your attitude permeates your entire approach to life. What does it cost you to start from a point of thinking there are more things going *for* you than going against you? What a fantastic foundation to build your attitude upon.

Albert Einstein is supposed to have said, "Weakness of attitude becomes weakness of character." A good attitude can't exist without basic self-esteem, because if you don't value yourself, how can you truly understand what it is to value anything or anybody else? Self-esteem can't exist without self-discipline. By that I don't mean you have to become a monk or a yogi; self-discipline begins by you alone taking responsibility for your actions. After you start creating true self-esteem, you inherently understand that others have value. And in understanding the value of others, you never, ever, underestimate or disrespect an adversary.

Ask yourself, What attitude am I approaching this situation with? Am I treating everyone I come in contact with as playing an important role in the accomplishment of my chosen goal? If a situation is not going well, check your attitude. What effect is the way I am approaching this having on the experience? Remember that example from Hell Week. The situation was difficult, but just a slight shift in my attitude created by my forced smile changed the outcome. When I deal with people, this is the first place I want to start. When I ignore the advantage a can-do attitude brings, I usually pay dearly.

D: Desire. How badly do you want it? It's got to provoke some feeling inside: Does it make your heart race? Or, does it bring you a feeling of peace? Do you feel exhilarated? I can remember how I felt after two weeks of plowing through snow and sleet with a ninety-six-pound pack strapped to my back, hearing the ice break off my body as I realized there was still twenty more miles of mountainous terrain to cover. The desire not to quit kept my feet moving. *I didn't let the mountain beat me, I beat the mountain.*

Whatever the case may be, only go after that which you truly desire. Otherwise, the odds are good that you won't have the energy it takes to see it through to the end, because nothing is ever as easy as it looks. Setting yourself up for failure is the worst thing you can do, because it undermines your belief in yourself. For instance, don't start working out because you think you should lose weight, or because you read it in a magazine. Do it because it is going to create value in your life by allowing you to participate, function in the world with more endurance and power. Work inside out, rather than outside in.

Think of desire as the rocket fuel that gets everything off the ground and propels you into places that have seemed otherwise unreachable. The desire not to quit has been my fuel for almost everything.

V: Visualization. The more clearly I visualize the results, the closer it is to being accomplished. I literally would see little pictures of myself as being a SEAL, like diving under the water in full combat swimmer gear . . . but I hadn't done that yet. I knew I could do the job if I could make it through Hell Week and the rest of BUD/S, because I had already seen it.

In Bukido we create this thing called "the Mind Lab," where it is the students' assignment to create an imaginary attacker. At first it's awkward; they have a hard time seeing that attacker, but we break it down so that one little piece of the picture at a time comes into focus. At first it appears to them like still pictures in a photo album, but then I start asking them questions to fill in the details: How is the attacker's arm moving? Where is this happening, in a house, on the street? Is he holding a weapon, and if so what does it look like? Eventually the pictures build into a slide show, then start moving as if in a film, and then, finally, it's almost a virtual reality experience, where the students feel they are in that environment face-to-face with the attacker. The students are eventually able to take their attacker and put him in any situation, in any environment, so that they are able to "practice" in the Mind Lab. Learning to see the relevant details allows you to anticipate correctly.

Whenever I needed to absolutely relax when I was working in the teams, I would go to this mountain retreat I had created in my mind. In this mountain retreat there was a pristine lake, and it was always summertime at this mountain retreat. I'd always go and sit down by the lake, which was calm and flat. The air was cool but comfortable. I could feel the life of nature around me, but nothing would disturb this moment. I would take a small pebble, throw it in the lake, and watch the ripples until they disappeared and the lake was smooth as glass again. By the time I finished this mental image, my body would always be completely relaxed, my mind clear. I don't go there as much as I did because now I have other tools that are simpler and get results faster. I do visit it sometimes, but now all I need to do to achieve that calm is watch the ripples until they disappear.

To create your own mental picture, start with your breath. In Bukido we have a "combat commandment" that says, "I will always remember that breathing is the skill that keeps the mind calm and the body strong during adversity." Here's a simple visualization exercise that also can help you relax. You can do it standing up or sitting down, before a board meeting or before asking somebody out on a date: Take "one Mississippi" to breathe in. Feel the breath completely fill your lungs. See the air rushing into the lungs. Hold it for another one. Imagine all the tension in your body entering your lungs and mixing with the air you have just inhaled. Then, exhale out for one and with that outgoing breath will go all the tension in your body. At first, take "three Mississippis" to complete the cycle, but the more often you do it you'll find the longer you'll want to and be able to stretch out each part of the cycle.

A: Attention. Bring your complete attention to what it is that you are doing. Remember, you can only solve one problem at a time. There is no way to solve all of your problems or difficulties at the same time. Attention is not about the past or the future, it is about the moment you're living right *now.*

N: Necessity. Define what is absolutely necessary and do it to the best of your ability. Edit your actions so that you keep only what is absolutely necessary. Write them down so that you can have an objective list of what you need to do. Chances are, when you see it all written down, there will be a few things that are redundant. Cross them off.

T: Timing. There are a few things to consider in regard to this. One is just about being on time: When conducting an ambush in SEAL Team, we are conditioned to understand that you can be several hours early but you can't afford to be one minute late. Another is about pacing yourself: Sometimes life requires you to sprint, other times it is an endurance event. Cross-train your mind so that you can be patient and flexible.

Timing is something that confuses many people. I break it up in two ways: There is time that is *wasted* and time that is *spent*. Wasted time is when you're moving and doing things where nothing gets accomplished. There are people who will waste your time, there are things and events that will do it, too. Our time on this planet is measured, not indefinite. You have to make a decision about whether you want to waste time or spend time. Relaxing and enjoying yourself is not wasted time, even if it is spent watching a silly TV show that you really want to see.

In Bukido, this concept of wasting time and spending time is talked about in terms of ratios. Because I was a sniper, the importance of one shot, one kill is conditioned in my mind as the most efficient use of time, resources, and energy. This means that all the time I spend to prepare and position myself to get to a specific target, no matter how long or laborious, is worth the single effort of pulling the trigger to get that single result of a target falling down. This means for every specific action I take, I get a specific result, always moving closer and closer to the end objective.

We strive to make every move count toward knocking down a given target. A 1:1 ratio would be where I move once and seriously damage or cause chaos on the attacker. It is important to know that just because an attacker moves first, it doesn't necessarily mean he strikes first. If the attacker's body has to move three times before he can damage a target on me (a 3:1 ratio), and I only have to move once with a very simple technique that causes a lot of damage to him (a 1:1 ratio), then I will strike first. When an attacker moves earlier with a technique that is more complicated, no matter how dangerous his chosen attack might be, his strike will be slower because it takes more time to perform. This is the reason we say that you can react later with a fast (simple) technique than earlier with a slow (more complicated) technique. A fast, effective technique uses time much better then a slow, effective technique. So even if I move slightly later than the attacker, I am employing a technique that uses time more efficiently. I will arrive at my target before he does.

In SEAL Team we cannot afford to waste time on operations; to ensure this we schedule it, in some cases, down to the second. One of the tools we use to properly schedule each phase involved in a mission is called a Phase Diagram. The Phase Diagram allows us to clearly and independently see each phase of the mission and how it flows in relation to timed objectives. To properly construct a Phase Diagram, we start from the point at which the primary target has to be knocked down. From this point we first work backward in time, including every detail that is involved and the time it takes to perform each detail. Once this is completed, it comes down to scheduling each phase—from after you have knocked down the target until you're back home and safely in the shower. Any set time restrictions, difficulties, and contingencies must be included within the flow chart of the Phase Diagram. (See p. 157.)

A: Alliances. Do I have allies? If not, how do I get some? Alliances begin with you extending yourself. When I think about alliances I think about value for value: You need to give something in order to get, even if what you have to give is as simple as a thank-you. The military practically defines the term "structure," but to exist within it, as with any huge system, you have to learn the difference between the strict flow chart of official organization and the unofficial, personal system of how things actually get done. I learned to treat everyone with the same amount of dignity and courtesy, because in practical application, the file clerk often had as much ability to get something done as the officer. I try to develop alliances with my students: From me they learn Bukido, from them I often gain new clients, suggestions about how to improve my business, good books to read, even clothes to buy. A friend once said to me, "It's not who you know, it's who knows you." Why make adversaries when you can make allies?

G: Gear. Do I have the appropriate equipment to get the job done? Gear in an everyday sense can mean your clothes, your computer, your car—anything that serves

Building a Phase Diagram

Begin constructing your Phase Diagram
from the moment you need to hit your target.

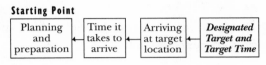

Build from your target to the starting point.

Starting Point

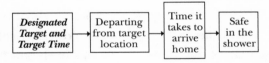

then

Build from your target to the finishing point.

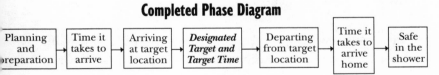

Build into each phase at least one contingency but no more than three. Be sure to pad some extra time into each phase as well. When opportunity is approaching you can afford to be early, but being one minute late could cost you everything.

Completed Phase Diagram

Planning and preparation	Time it takes to arrive	Arriving at target location	**Designated Target and Target Time**	Departing from target location	Time it takes to arrive home	Safe in the shower

Any phase that requires movement of some type must have at least two contingencies. Movement is where most plans run into the greatest problems.

to facilitate your actions. Any gear you have should be appropriate for the environment in which you're using it. More complicated is not necessarily better. Anything with a lot of parts has that much more that can go wrong with it. Use what you need, and forget the bells and whistles—they're usually nothing more than distractions anyway. Gear is an important idea that too often gets neglected—take care of your gear so that your gear takes care of you.

E: Emergency. If you don't have a backup in case things go wrong, you don't have a plan, period. What are you going to do, and how much do you have to do, to salvage the situation if it doesn't proceed as you envision it? At the very least, how are you going to make a safe exit?

S: Skills. As we talked about in the last chapter, acquiring new and better skills is a lifelong process. But in planning for the short term, you need to ask: Do I need new or better skills before I can tackle this, or will what I have now get me through? Assessing the situation ruthlessly will tell you where your skill level is. If I don't have the time or money to acquire new skills, I check my alliances to see if they can provide what I need. The better my skills, the more effective my actions.

Advantage stacking might begin as something you write down as a part of planning for how you'll knock down a target, but the more you use it you'll see that it becomes a general attitude, a way to approach life. The **ADVANTAGES** checklist is not only a part of everything I do in my business, it helped me get my business off the ground. In the not-too-distant past I had to present the idea of the Bukido Institute to three businessmen who had the means to make it possible for me to knock down the target. If they didn't buy the concept, I would be another two years away from my target. This is what I used to prepare for the meeting—and since you're reading this book right now, you already know the ending:

✓*Attitude:* Demonstrate absolute enthusiasm and confidence in the concept of having a central place where people can come to learn this system I have developed. What I have developed can be useful to people and can improve their safety, mental health, and life in general.

✓*Desire:* Do I really want this institute? Yes. Would I rather be doing something, anything else? No. Be prepared to demonstrate this desire in every action that I take.

✓*Visualization:* I see myself in a shirt that has the Bukido logo. I am teaching a small group of students who are intently focused on the lesson of the day. The room is clean, mirrors line the side, mats are placed throughout. Punching bags hang in one corner. I imagine seeing myself interviewed in magazines, returning phone calls from people interested in Bukido, having a checking account with the corporate name on it.

✓*Attention:* There are a few other projects in the wings but I won't pursue them now because to do so would dilute my focus. My complete attention has to be focused on this target.

✓*Necessity:* Do I really need to have a place? Yes. Without it I don't have the credibility I need to knock down the secondary targets I have lined up behind it. Do I really need this meeting or can I do it some other way? No. An in-the-flesh presentation will make an impression they won't be able to pass up.

✓ *Timing:* Has there been enough demand to warrant growing my business? Yes. Is this the right time to meet with the investors? Have they lost money recently on a similar idea? No indication of that. Is a morning meeting the best? Yes. If they like what they hear the meeting can maybe extend over into lunch. The more time I have, the better. Can I perform reliably right now? Yes.

✓ *Alliances:* Have other friends in business look over the proposal for potential problems. Ask students for their testimonials to put in the proposal. Establish a good rapport with the club where I want to rent space. When I get to their offices for the meeting, be kind and courteous to everyone I meet. Treat everyone as a potential ally.

✓ *Gear:* Do I have the proposal well organized with diagrams, sales figures, competing business information, etc.? Is more information readily available? Yes. Do I have a suit that makes me look like a man who can handle money? Yes.

✓ *Emergency:* What happens if I get shot down before I can even make my case? What will I say as I exit? Can I make do with what I have going now until another opportunity comes along, or do I need to look for another venture?

✓ *Skills:* Can I effectively present the proposal or do I need to practice my pitch? I can present it. I've practiced to the point where I could present the thing backward. Would it be worthwhile to have others chime in? No. Do I know how to be a good instructor and promote business? Is the Pope Catholic?

It may seem simple, but the attitude of stacking advantages in my favor has gotten me through some of the most complicated, and dangerous, things I have ever had to face.

Everything you have learned so far has ultimately been about stacking advantages in your favor. But I want you to really be confident that these principles work, even under the most physically stressful conditions, when lives are really on the line. This was the environment they were born out of, where they were tested and honed. Now I'm going to take you on a SEAL mission so you can see all the principles of this book put into action. Are you up for it?

Let's go.

The mission appears, at face value, to be straightforward. Our *mission* will be to take black-and-white photos of a hangar. Except, that means the hangar is located in a place where pictures can't be taken by either aerial photography or satellites. And let's just say that also means there are a lot of not-so-nice people dead set against us seeing what's inside that particular hangar. So if we're going to get a shot of it, we have to do it in the pitch black of night.

I'm the point man in our squad, but because I am also the intelligence representative and I have been trained in extreme night photography, I'm also charged with the duty of bringing an image out of complete blackness. Meaning, I'm supposed to capture an image *I can't see.*

The seven of us on this operation are flying at night in a huge C130 Galaxy aircraft. Camouflage uniforms cover our wet suits, over which we each wear a static line parachute with a belly reserve. Diving fins are taped to my shins, just as they are to everybody else's. I see my team-mates by the glow of red lights that run across the inside top of the aircraft's bulkhead. It is dark but I can see that some guys are napping while others are keeping their thoughts busy. Maybe they're thinking about the mission, or about their loved ones, or maybe just about the pizza they're going to devour when we get back.

I look into the belly of the plane and see two inflat-able black boats, called combat rubber raiding crafts, placed on top of each other. They then are tied onto a 1,500-pound wooden platform loaded with sandbags so the boats will fall flat through the air and land upright in the water. Inside the boats are engines, weapons, and backpacks, everything we need to get the op started right. The whole package is then connected to a gigantic G-12 parachute. Completed it is called a stacked rubber duck.

The chief petty officer stands up; before he became a chief they used to call him "Boats" because he is the epit-ome of a sailor—flick his ears and salt comes off. He smacks each of us on the head to get us to *attention* as he moves to the rear of the aircraft to check the Duck.

"Five minutes!" he yells while lifting up his right hand to give us a visual—four fingers and a thumb. He proceeds to examine the duck one last time.

Butterflies flutter in the stomach; the signal that *fear* is creeping up. I'm in fact getting ready to hurl my body out of this plane as it cruises 1,200 feet above the ground, just enough space for the parachutes to open. I use my standard *Verbal Command Request* for these situations: I know what I'm doing. I want to be here.

A large ramp in the back starts to drop; we can hear the hydraulic motors of the C130's ramp drop down. The red light in the back of the aircraft next to the rear exit comes on. I can see moonlight shining on the black water.

The chief yells, "Hook *up!*" while giving us the appropriate hand signal. We click the metal hooks of our static lines onto a thick wire cable, then stick a pin into a tiny hole that locks the hook on the cable. Chief taps his head, the cue to check your equipment. We do a quick inspection. I check my buddy in front to make sure his lines are in proper place and there is no gear hanging off of him that could lead to any kind of a malfunction. My buddy behind me does the same for me. We're ready to jump.

Chief looks back and yells, "Two minutes!" with two fingers appropriately raised. We respond, and each show our two fingers to the man in front and the man behind us. We start to tighten our "stick," a straight formation. I watch the other guys running malfunctions checks. Chief sticks his head out of the ramp to make sure we're on course, throwing out a streamer to check the wind. The skin on his face ripples from the force of 130-knot winds. He looks back and smiles. We are going.

He stands up, steps to the rear, hooks up his static line. He taps the guy in front to let him know he is all set, and like dominos the taps run all the way up to me, the one in front. I inch up closer to the duck; the stick tightens again, the light turns green. Chief reaches over and pulls the quick release on the duck.

It takes off. I move out to be right next to it. The stick follows quickly, because if we don't stay close to the duck, we won't be anywhere near it when it hits the water.

As the parachute on the duck comes out, I jump into blackness, immediately getting into a tight, tucked, parachute body position, so that 130-mile-an-hour winds don't just toss me and tangle the chute. One-one thousand, two-one thousand, three-one thousand, four—

The chute bursts open. The leg straps that run along the sides of my groin jerk together as my body comes to an instant halt. The pain that is caused is a welcome relief, there is no doubt that the chute has been deployed. I look up to check my canopy to make sure the chute is good. Then . . . where's the duck?

There it is. I look right and left, and count the parachutes. Six, plus me, means we are all here. My job is to get to the duck first and cut the rigging that will set them free. But I can't think about that yet because that's my *secondary target*. My *primary target* is hitting the water.

I undo the belly band on my reserve chute and unlatch the left side of my reserve. I swing it away from me to the right. I reach up and unclip my chest strap. I do this so that I don't get tangled up in the harness of the parachute when I enter the water. Now the only two things holding me into this parachute as I fall from the sky are the two leg straps clipped on my hips. I undo the quick releases on my fins and slide them over my boots. My fins are on; a thought flashes over my mind: "Got to get the boats set up quick so we can set up the navigation compasses and minimize the drift in the ocean."

But I can't think about that right now.

First things first. Land in the water. There are maybe fifty feet left. I am right next to the duck. So far so good.

At ten feet, I unclip my leg straps, then fall into the ocean. The cold shocks my body and makes me catch my breath. I've go to focus on the target in front of me. I look around to make sure that I am clear of the parachute in the water. I've got to get the chute gathered together and let it sink so nobody else gets tied in it—and so nobody else ever finds it.

I swim quickly to the duck. The current is a little swifter than I thought; got to get the next phase done quickly. I hear someone swimming up next to me; I know it's one of my guys. My swim buddy and I climb onto the duck. I look for the donut, the piece where the two boats can be tied together. I have to do this with no lights and go by feel alone. I know what to do because I've rehearsed it so many times with my eyes closed.

I pull my knife out, the only one that is pulled out during this entire procedure. This is our *Standard Operating Procedure.* Two knives would be faster, but that also doubles the chance that one of the boats could be accidentally punctured. I reach for the donut.

"Cutting lines," I say, warning everyone that there's the danger of cutting lines under tension. I slice it. The lines snap away. My swim buddy finds the other donut— when that gets cut, the wooden pallet will drop away.

"Clear pallet," I say, and I cut the last donut.

Half the pallet slides away while the other half of it is still tied to the boat.

What's going on? What happened?

I have to find out why. At this point, if someone gets tied up in those loose nylon lines and the pallet comes loose, they could get dragged underwater. This has to be fixed now. I am also painfully aware that the current is pulling us off course.

Chief swims over to ask me what's taking so long—except, he doesn't say it like that.

"Give me two seconds," I reply. I close my eyes. I reach one hand to the side of the boat, trying to find where the line is tied. There is a tight stressed line wrapped around some others.

I reach down. It leads into the water; I know this is the one holding the pallet up. "Clear line!"

Nylon line under stress *dictates* the weapon: knife. *The weapon dictates the movement:* Turn the knife edge so that the line can be cut in a motion that goes away from the rubber boat.

I protect my face from the tension in the line as I cut it with my knife. The pallet drops and disappears in the water.

Three *targets* down, 150 more already lined up.

We have a thirty-mile transit in the ocean with twelve five-gallon gasoline bladders. More than enough gas to get us where we need to go. *Advantage stacking.* That doesn't leave much room for gear. Good thing this is a reconnaissance mission. If it was a direct-action mission—meaning, if we had to destroy something—we'd need a lot more gear. We have to be out of here by sunrise. We have to make it back to a submarine ten miles out, or we'll be making the evening news.

We are ten minutes behind schedule, according to

the *phase diagram* we built during our planning. We have seven hours left to get this op done. No mission ever goes as perfectly as planned. The secret is to plan thoroughly so that you can perform reliably. Effectiveness first, efficiency second.

My *intuition* radar is going off—I need to make the course correction in my head, because I just feel in my gut that our satellite navigation system is off by a hair. I navigated us onto beaches for years before we ever got these electronic navigation aids. They are helpful in double-checking the route, but I don't rely on them exclusively.

I check my compass bearing and find out my intuition was right. We're off.

Chief and the lieutenant are not happy with what's going on, their faces show concern. Whenever they rely on one of their men to take charge, they put a lot on the line. Sometimes it is their careers, and sometimes it is the very lives of their men. But while it's difficult for them to rely on an enlisted man, they know that the small size of our unit means they have to trust the man with the best experience. The man that has their trust better not screw up. One screwup will destroy a thousand "at-a-boys."

"I have an idea," I say.

"You better be right," the chief says.

"No problem," I say, but I'm not feeling absolutely convinced.

I rely on my senses and good experience: I make the course correction.

The *primary target* that is now solely on my mind is getting to the beach on the right spot. Nothing else matters. The right spot on the beach offers cover for us to conceal our movement to the next target. We also don't want the ocean to crash us into the rocks. This operation becomes ten times more difficult if we don't get to the right point on the beach.

The weather is good and we make up ten minutes. The Frog God—passed down from the combat demolition units in WW II, known as Frogmen, the grandfathers of the SEALs—must be with us.

Two guys bring us just outside of the surf zone and stay in the boats as five of us swim 700 yards to the beach with our gear. That water is cold. I think about the camera. Has any water gotten into the camera case? Did I put the silicone lubrication on the seals of the camera case? I know I did. I better have. I can't think about the possibility of failure right now. *Attitude.*

What I've got to think about is the weather. Frog God was nice to give us good weather to get onto the beach, but guess what? Good weather makes the beach and brush very dry. Not good for sneaking. Getting to the hangar might take some time. We might lose again the ten minutes we just made up. We may even lose hours.

Five guys moving through dry brush sounds like a heard of wild elephants stampeding. Lieutenant knows this. He quickly *assesses the situation* after we travel 500 yards into the hinterland, that area just beyond the beach. The lieutenant powwows with me and the chief and *creates a simple plan.* A tough decision is made: Lieutenant does not want to split up the men, but we can't move fast enough with five guys. It comes down to me and the lieutenant. Bad for us if we make a mistake. This is much more dangerous for us, but overall the men are safer because we can now move more smoothly and stealthily. This is not what we planned. We just reduced our firepower by more than half but increased our chances to complete the mission successfully. *Assess the situation. Create a simple plan. Take action. Evaluate your progress.*

Chief is not happy. Lieutenant and I take off. *Take action.*

We have about a mile to go before we get to the next target, the place where we take the photo. My job right now is to watch for booby traps, listen for the things that don't belong, keep clear of trails, and navigate. Lieutenant keeps our pace count and makes the major decisions.

We have to slow down because we're making too much noise. In some places we are forced to crawl under brush, and in others we must slowly step inch by inch, with our feet moving over dry, brittle branches and leaves. It is much more difficult to move stealthily at night than you might think. For one thing, it's hard to see where you're going. I know guys who have stepped off small slopes because they couldn't even see their hand in front of their face. The other reason is that people can hear better at night. Think about it: All of the ambient noise that happens in the daylight, like birds chirping or cars driving by, dies. Not to mention the fact that people by nature are diurnal. *Accuracy comes before speed.*

I walk into a large spiderweb that covers my face. A good-size spider is moving from my cheek toward my neck. As a kid I was practically arachnophobic—one of the reasons I wanted to be a point man was to completely get over that fear, because the point man is always first to hit the webs. What an exercise in *walking through your fear* and getting to the other side. Now I reach up, grab the spider, and toss it away.

I check my watch. We've eaten up an hour and a half going just a mile.

Finally, we reach the hangar. We're at the point where we have to pick the best place to take a photo. We do this all with hand signals. During the entire trip we haven't said one word to one another.

Now the whole op comes down to me. No one can help me, no one can give me advice, no one can overrule me. It now all comes down to, Can I bring an image I cannot see onto film that I cannot develop until I get back on the submarine?

No big deal, right?

Slowly, I bring the pack around to my front. I have zippers on the pack because Velcro would be too loud. I can hear the sand in the zippers grating. To me it sounds like a bulldozer. When the zipper is fully opened, I slowly but deliberately remove the camera case from the bag. I do this with eyes closed to concentrate fully. This is the way I practiced a thousand times. *Perfect practice.* My eyes can deceive me at night but my mind won't, so I *visualize* what has to be done. Lieutenant points at his watch. He gives me only half an hour to get this job done. *Timing.*

I open the case. Everything inside the case is preset for this moment. I even have two cameras. *Gear.* There is a SEAL axiom that states, "Two is one and one is none." That's *advantage stacking.*

I have to stealthily extend the aluminum legs of the tripod without making any noise. I have to screw the

Canon F-1 camera onto it. I double-check the individual settings to make sure they are where I want them. *Know your gear.* The f-stop, or lens aperture, has to be fully open, the focus ring on the lens has to be set on infinity, and the shutter speed must be placed on bulb setting to control the speed of the shutter manually. I screw the cable release into the shutter release. This is all completed with my eyes closed. *I just concentrate on the correct fundamentals.* I have to calculate the different time exposures in my head. The more light I let in on that film, the more I burn that image onto the film. That's why we are here.

Lieutenant keeps a watchful eye out for sentries. The opening and closing of the camera's shutter sounds like a guillotine to me. I could almost swear the sound can be heard from a mile away.

All of a sudden, we hear a guard approach. We stop cold. He walks within a hundred feet of our position. From the way he's walking it's obvious the guard feels comfortable in his surroundings. He sounds like a rhino. Lieutenant ever so slowly raises his CAR-15 rifle with suppressor. He points it at the guard.

We don't even breathe. Did he hear us? Does he see us?

It seems like an hour goes by as he walks past us. I am definitely aware of the passing time.

Four more exposures to go, just in case.

Click. They are long exposures. *Click.*

Once the exposures are done, I feel a tremendous wave of pressure wash over me. I really won't know if I've done everything right until we get back to the sub and develop the pictures. Have I done everything right? Have I

wasted everybody's time, money—or lives? These thoughts
are the fear talking. *This is the verbal-influence conditioning
that leads to feelings of panic.* I have to move past it. I must
rely on my training and use a *Verbal Command Request* that
moves me forward to the next target.

I must get focused, this is the point in an operation
where you can get sloppy in your thinking. We've accomplished the main objective but this mission is far from finished. I have to be focused in the now.

With the same slow, methodical movements, I return
every single thing back to its original location. The new
primary target is to not leave a shred of evidence behind.
No one can ever know we have been here. I go through
my preplanned mental checklist. Everything is back in its
designated place.

The next target is to link back up with the guys. It
takes an hour to get back, putting us about a half hour
behind schedule. When we arrive at our rally point, the
lieutenant takes out a small pin light that has a red filter
covering it. We get to our spot. He flashes the red light
three times. We wait.

No response.

He does it again. Nothing.

We look at each other. Did the chief feel that we
weren't going to make it back on time? No way, there is
nothing on earth that could make the chief leave some of
his boys behind. Lieutenant closes his eyes. Maybe he is
praying. He opens them, then sends three quick flashes. If
we can't link up with the chief, then we will have to act on
our secondary extraction plan. Which means that me and
the lieutenant could end up spending a week hiding in

enemy territory waiting for our next opportunity to extract. *This was our contingency in case of an emergency.*

At last we get three flashes in return. Lieutenant and I walk to where the red light was flashing. Lieutenant whispers, "Eight." Chief whispers in reply, "Three." This is the challenge and reply, so we know we're talking to each other and not an enemy in disguise. It could be any combination as long as it equals eleven.

The linkup is complete. We head to the beach.

Chief looks at me. I give him a thumbs-up. He gives me one nod. That nod says, You better have gotten the shot. I don't dwell on failure, because it is not an option.

We are hustling now—we've got a sub to catch.

We hit the beach. Twenty minutes later, we are through the surf zone and onto the boats. We are moving out.

One hour and fifteen minutes remain for us to go ten miles. That cuts it tight. I'm glad that we're not loaded down with a ton of gear, because dawn is coming. If the sun breaks the horizon, the sub won't surface and we will be exposed like ducks on a pond.

Our radio man tries to make contact to let the sub know we are on our way to the extraction point—the place where we will be picked up.

I check our bearings, make sure we are headed on the right course.

Half hour down. I can feel dawn coming. Like Dracula, we could all be dead if the sun gets to us.

Then it happens. Second only to being shot at, the worst thing that can happen when traveling in a small boat when you want to get someplace is that the engine on the other boat dies. This engine failure would be disastrous if we hadn't planned for it. The lieutenant had wanted to bring a spare engine for a single boat, but the chief asked him, "Why should we just bring a spare engine when we could bring a completely spare boat for the same effort?" Since the lieutenant is a very smart man, he listened to his chief.

We transfer the gear and gas bladders to our boat. Chief and his swim buddy stab all of the air tubes, then jump into our boat. We watch to make sure that the useless engine dragged the deflated boat under the ocean.

Chief leans over. "Mack, did you get the @#!$ shots?"

I want to say, "I don't know," but that ain't an option. So I say, "Yes, Chief." I am thankful that I have trained this skill over and over again, always trying to find a better, cleaner, more efficient way to perform it. *Consistency*.

No contact on the radio yet. Five minutes till we stop the boat. And we are not even close to being finished. I look at my watch. Sunrise is at 6:00. It's 5:50 right now.

We have two more minutes of driving. Still no sign of the sub.

We stop the boats, put the engine on idle, and sit there, floating at sea. We can still see land—that means we can be seen. They can see us if they are looking . . . and intelligence sources say they routinely watch the ocean. Eventually, they will be looking, but when and how soon?

Two minutes go by. It will take seven minutes just to reload the gear and boats onto the sub. Radio man tries one more time. Ten minutes till dawn.

Chief looks at me. Lieutenant looks at me.

"We're in the right spot," I say.

"We better be," the chief replies.

He looks back, checks the navigation.

Radio man tries again. Nothing.

Eight minutes till dawn.

Then, two hundred meters to our right, the water looks like it's boiling. A periscope comes out of the water. My heart nearly leaps out of my chest. We have seven minutes left.

We race over to the sub. It breaks the surface like a city on the ocean.

But we're not in the showers yet. . . . The nervous energy disappears and in its place is focused energy, like lasers. The other half of the platoon is on the sub throwing down lines to drag our packs and equipment on board. A Jacob's ladder is lowered for us to climb up.

The sky is turning purple, threads of pink hint at the horizon. The stars are fading. The boats are rolled up and stowed in the deck lockers.

We file into the sub, climbing down the porthole of the sub's tower. I follow the engine through and down the porthole. The last person on deck is the sub's officer. I look up at him and it's like looking up through a well. The sky behind him is blue now. He pulls the hatch closed, sealing it.

We disappear.

And by the way—we got the shots.

Chapter 7

Never Grow Complacent

Tomorrow is the most important thing in life.
Comes into us at midnight very clean.
It's perfect when it arrives and puts itself in our
    hands.
It hopes we've learned something from yesterday.

—John Wayne

I t was a perfect Malibu night. The hot summer day had turned cool and comfortable thanks to the light ocean breeze. The grounds of the Spanish-style mansion sprawled over most of a hill overlooking the Pacific. And the stars were out in record number.

The five hundred or so guests who were attending this $5,000-a-plate benefit for a local Los Angeles charity didn't have to walk up any stairs on the steep property. They checked in their limousines and a trolley was provided to bring them from the gardens below up to the catered white tent. Inside the tent, giant ice sculptures decorated a buffet filled with nouvelle cuisine, with shrimp the size of bananas and lobster freshly pulled from the water. Champagne fountains flowed, the tables were set with white linens and silver, and the live band included some well-known R&B artists whose music I'd loved hearing on the radio growing up. The guests filling the dance floor looked like a veritable Who's Who of pop culture—an Oscar-nominated actress rubbing shoulders with a television news anchor, a record producer laughing at a joke from a sitcom star.

I'd arrived several hours before the event to check the property, looking for weak links—any areas not totally secure—that might be just what a stalker, or the paparazzi, would need to crash the event. After supervising the guest check-in, my job for the rest of the night would be to shadow a man whose boyish charm, rugged good looks, and crystal blue eyes make him one of the biggest box office draws in the world. If he has any problems, all he has to do is look over his shoulder and I'll know what to do. But with my black Armani suit and perfect shave, well, I look like any other Hollywood wannabe-type and just blend into the background.

The "blending in" was obviously working. The reputation California women have for being some of the most attractive on the planet is certainly well deserved, and a couple of them were attempting to engage me in conversation. I was thinking, This is a pretty good deal. I'd been in California less than three months. But, here I was, already at the epicenter of glamour, making more money than I had ever even seen in my life, having a beautiful redhead slip me a note to meet her later at the Marmalade Cafe, and being fed a gourmet meal. It was a far cry from "mystery meatloaf" and corn, being stuck in a submarine for a month with two hundred smelly guys, getting up at 4:00 A.M. to crawl through mud and sewage, and, just maybe, get shot at. Tonight the most serious threat I'd likely encounter was a Nikon-wielding *National Enquirer* reporter.

But something felt wrong.

I was flattered by the female attention, but really, why were they talking to me? They obviously didn't know my face, but because I was in the inside circle next to the star, it probably seemed as if I were "somebody" with a certain amount of Hollywood clout. Although I was near all this wealth and luxury, I was really just on the sidelines, watching other people live their lives. I realized at that moment I was facing the most dangerous threat of my life: the lure of comfort, the lure of "close enough." This wasn't anything like what I had always wanted to do, but with perks like this I could easily grow accustomed to a lucrative and comfortable life, and watch the years slide into decades.

It occurred to me that there are many other people who were more interested, more patient, and better suited to work in executive protection. It was not as if I had retired after a career in the police force or military and was looking for interesting times and some big paychecks to pay for my Baja sailing habit, as was the case for some of the top protection guys.

When I decided to sign up for my second enlistment in the SEALs, that's when I made the decision that, ultimately, there was more I was meant to do within the teams. I hadn't gathered enough skills. Although my evaluations said my work had been outstanding, I knew, deep within myself, that I had grown complacent. I knew what the job required, there were many times it was exciting and rewarding, but I had stopped looking for that next big hurdle. I felt I was coasting on past success. I managed to become a SEAL at age nineteen. I thought, What a great start to a life, but I didn't want my biggest accomplishment to forever be behind me. Because I was no longer the "skinny kid" and had carved out a niche for myself, I had forgotten there were plenty of challenges left for me. When I had to make the decision to sign up again, I had to face the fact that all I had done was widen my comfort zone—there was still a universe of knowledge and experience that it would take me five lifetimes to know, if I was open to them. I started focusing on developing a consistent set of principles so that I could become a better SEAL.

But, as I neared age thirty, something hadn't felt right about being in the military anymore, either. I had ten years under my belt as a SEAL, what most would consider halfway to retirement. Those ten years had seemed to pass in the blink of an eye, another ten years would probably do the same. I felt I wanted to create something uniquely my own, something I could share with the world. One of the hardest truths from my SEAL training came back to me: In war, if you grow complacent, you die. It's as simple as that.

Allowing yourself even a moment of complacency in the field signals the prelude to things going wrong. Leave behind a tiny piece of trash on a reconnaissance mission and you could get a whole battalion of marines or rangers, whose mission it is to take out that target after SEAL Team has set it up, killed. That one complacent act on your part can be the sign that tells the enemy that an American force was there watching them. Now on the alert, the enemy can set up an ambush for the U.S. force they now know is on the way.

Complacency is the first and easiest thing you can

allow in that it will screw up your life. It will kill marriages, friendships, careers, opportunities, dreams, and even entire societies.

By growing complacent, I was slowly quitting on myself. I've often met people who retire from an occupation they were really good at and then find themselves bored, miserable, and listless. It's as if you can actually see the life draining right out of them. Human beings need mountains to climb, we need frontiers to explore. We have to reach for the impossible, or something in us dies. The body might take years to catch up, but inevitably it follows the will.

Change is inevitable; seeking *improved* change is the hallmark of a developed being. Up to the point in my life when I left SEAL Team, I had been dedicated to the pursuit of being an ideal warrior, and I had to remind myself of all that meant: The mercenary fights for a buck, the soldier fights because he is ordered to, but the warrior fights for a cause. He doesn't fight for pettiness or mindless bloodshed. The warrior fights because he believes that he is fighting for something good, something positive, something that will improve the quality of the world around him. The warrior never forgets that he is the example and so will always remember to act accordingly. He is a leader, and when there is no one else to lead, the warrior must lead himself forward to a different, higher standard. The warrior knows that he cannot and will not hide the truth from himself, because to do so would be to breed weakness. The warrior knows if he chooses the weakest path, ultimately the person he truly cheats is himself.

The warrior understands the importance of discipline and understands fully that the highest, most valuable form of discipline is self-discipline. It is the only path that leads to mastery of any type. Discipline is not a gift you get at birth, it's not in your genes. It is simply doing something and sticking to it, even if you have to take it second by second. Every self-starter who has accomplished incredible success has had self-discipline over himself or herself at least to some degree. It may have been only over the subject that he or she felt passionately about, but that passion drove him or her to develop new and improved skills, to seek out new teachers and new innovations, to attempt to satisfy an unquenchable thirst for knowledge on the subject of his or her passion.

To choose the path of a warrior means you must develop an inextinguishable passion for life. When you do, the amazing value of it is always in the forefront of your mind and propels your body. In SEAL Team, when things looked the worst, when the mud was up to our ears, when the night was the coldest, when the mountain looked the highest, when the guns felt the hottest, the only way around it all was through it. "Get amongst it," we'd say.

This, above all, will unleash the warrior inside each of us. It's not enough to understand the principles in this book, we have to continuously apply them. Don't look for ways to get around life. Grab it, jump in it. Do something, anything, but *get amongst it*!

Acknowledgments

I don't know if I can adequately acknowledge all the people who taught me the lessons that are in this book, or that I learned while writing it. I know in my heart that I'll never be able to thank them all the way they should be thanked. But I will attempt, in some small way, to do so.

I can't thank my agent, Neeti Madan, enough. She is incredible and talented. I would also like to thank Peter Matson and the other professionals at Sterling Lord Literistic for all their suggestions and encouragement.

To my editor, David Cashion, thank you for believing in this project, giving me the freedom to create it, and being available when I needed you. I am proud to be published by the hardworking people of Hyperion, and to be a part of the Disney family.

To the woman who provided the spark that got this whole thing ablaze, Renée Vogel, thank you for everything you did to help this turn out right. Thanks to Mary Rakow and Lola Willoughby for taking the time to carefully read this work in its earliest incarnations and helping to model it into a work that I am proud of. Thank you, Laurie Steiner, for your amazing photos;

they helped in every step of the process. Thanks to John Buksbazen for helping me to articulate in a simple way what I tend to make complicated. John, I really appreciate your friendship.

It was my distinct pleasure to work and serve with all the men of BUD/S Class 136, Alpha, Golf and Hotel Platoons, and the training cadres of SEAL Team One and Two. You guys taught me a lot. I would like to send specific thanks to the following: James Madson, Don Shipley, Vincent Napple, Tim Farrell, Chuck Williams, Randy Paulus, Andy Nelson, Joe Macguire, Joseph Kernan, Thomas Richards, Tom Brown, Brian Zinke, Rock Blais, Todd Seniff, Steve Decker, Boyd Renner, Kevin Holderby, and Frank Odermann. These men taught me some of my biggest lessons in the Teams and in life—some of which I didn't want to learn. You *all* helped a boy become a man.

I would like to send David Soulé a special thanks for showing me how a professional scout/sniper/SEAL looks and acts. A special acknowledgment to the late, great Gunnery Sergeant Carlos N. Hathcock II (USMC) for his contributions to the NSW scout/sniper program. He did much more than teach men how to shoot; he taught them how to survive in the field. John Shaw developed a series of programs at his institute that taught me so much more than just how to shoot. And a special thank-you to the SEALs who served in Vietnam: It's off of your awesome reputation I lived for a decade.

It is important to acknowledge that the reconnaissance mission in chapter 6 is an amalgamation of both "real-world" and operational exercises. I tried hard to exclude any information that would give away any actual SEAL operational tactics, field strategies, or standard operational procedures currently in use by SEAL Team. There are men out there in the long, dark, cold night busting their asses to do a very demanding job without me making it any more difficult for them. As for all of the other military stories, they are told as closely to the facts as I can best remember. Students of the Bukido Institute sign a nondisclosure agreement that states they will not give out specific information about the program and that the institute will not discuss them in a public forum. It is for this reason that almost all of their names and anecdotes have been altered to conceal their identities.

To the professionals who have guided, supported, or shared some of their knowledge with me after SEAL Team: Edward Dugan, John Quinn, Blair Gluba, John Cox, Jerry Glazebrook, Larry Nicholson, James Stalnaker, Joesph Paskvan, Fred Foster, and Kurt Angel. To Rod Koyne, one cool, hard-charger who I always managed to drag into trouble. And to Avi Korein, who led me to choose between following a dream and something that I was merely interested in. These men have forgotten more about professionally protecting people and assets than I'll ever learn.

I owe a debt of gratitude to many men for the ways in which they have influenced my thinking on the martial arts: the instructors of the NSW Combat Fighting Instructor Course (for finding the best instructors in the world to teach us); Paul Vunack; Frank Cucci; the Gracie family; Tony Blauer; Bruce Chiu; Danny Isanto; and, of course, Bruce Lee. To each I give thanks for contributing, either directly or indirectly, to my diversified learning. And to the lady who made me rethink everything that I ever learned, Donna Johnson, thank you.

I want to thank Lisa Hockley, Ray Byers, Aaron Tolchin, Jeremy Wieand, Brett Zebrowski, and the fantastic staff at the Fitness Forum in Marina Del Rey. I really appreciate the professionalism and courteous and respectful nature with which you deal with me, the Bukido staff, and our clients. What an amazing facility.

To John Wilson, who brought to my attention how much Bukido training was really worth. His help and guidance were instrumental in the Bukido Institute taking off. To the hard-charging members of Team Bukido: Christopher Hicks, Stephanie Robertson, Steve Lee, and Jean-Claude Pagnal. Each of you deserves more thank-yous than I could say in a lifetime. Your hard work and tireless dedication are an example to me. I would also like to express my appreciation to all of my students for their constant encouragement.

To Sharon and Gordon Rorick, thank you for opening your home and hearts to me when I first arrived in California. It is great to have you as part of my extended family.

And, lastly, to four people who helped me in ways I'll never be able to express fully. It is barely scratching the surface to say that without them this target could not have been knocked down. To my mom, Patricia Patrick, who always wanted me to follow my dream and do what I love. I love you, Mom. To Welton and Carol Whann, I can't express the depth of my affection for you. I am so proud to be included in your family. And, lastly, to Samantha Dunn, who went through hell just to help me set up this target, not to even mention the journey we went on to knock it down. It is to you that I owe this fulfilled dream. You're one of a kind.

Appendix

This exercise was designed for you to apply your understanding of the Three Dynamic Elements of Combat. But to do this, you will use an amalgamation of the principles in the book to create and define specific weapons and their accompanying movement to take out your target.

Pick one target that you really want to knock down.

Target: _____

_____

_____

Define at least five weapons that will help you knock down this target. Your weapons inventory should include the following as a guide:

1. Allies (who can help you and how can you help them?):

_____

_____

_____

2. Skill acquisition (training):

_____

_____

_____

3. A to-do list (basic schedule planning):

_____

_____

_____

4. Gear (equipment):

_____

_____

_____

5. Desire (how bad do you want this target?):

_____

_____

_____

Explain how you will use each weapon to knock down your target. Take your time on this part, include details but avoid over-complicating how you will move. When addressing the weapon in this example, connect it directly to your chosen target. This is to always remind you that you are using this weapon to knock down a specific target.

Weapon One:

_____

_____

_____

Weapon Two:

_____

_____

_____

Weapon Three:

_____

_____

_____

Weapon Four:

_____

_____

_____

Weapon Five:

_____

_____

_____

_____

Glossary

ACTE™: Acronym that stands for *A*ssess the situation; *C*reate a simple plan; *T*ake action; and *E*valuate your progress.

Action Mind-set: The process of recognizing and moving beyond your fear to completely focus on what is known.

Action Trigger: A specifically constructed Verbal Command Request that propels you into action.

Advantage-Stacking Thought Process: A strategic thought process developed to stack so many advantages in your favor that when you take action, you can't help but win.

ADVANTAGES™: An acronym that stands for Attitude; Desire; Visualization; Attention; Necessity; Timing; Alliances; Gear; Emergency; Skills. It is the starting point for questions that, when answered, stack advantages in your favor.

Basic Underwater Demolition/SEAL Training (BUD/S): The primary training course that must be passed for an individual to be considered eligible for a SEAL Team.

Berm: A large sand pile that stretches for miles and acts as a sea break during heavy storms.

Bukido™: A word created from Japanese characters to describe the journey an individual must take to bring out the "warrior within."

Bukido Training System™: A symbiosis of mental and physical disciplines that develop skills for use under extreme stress and in the accomplishment of goals. A philosophy of performance, not a philosophy of ideology.

CARVER matrix: The process that allows an individual to clearly evaluate the priority ranking of a given set of targets. The matrix also tells the individual about the strengths and weaknesses inherent in each target evaluated.

Close-Quarter Battle (CQB): The clearing and securing of rooms that contain armed threats.

Dry firing: A practice professional shooters do to perfect the mechanics of their shooting technique. It is done only after the weapon is made completely safe, without ammunition.

80 Percent MAX: The point at which you use all of your abilities to 80 percent of your maximum potential. A place where your body and mind stay in balance and harmony, *to flow rather than force*. In sports performance, researchers call this the "steady state," because your body's systems are running at an efficient level.

Energy: The capacity of power or force available for action.

Evolution: A cycle or series of events involving the movement of troops, ships, and equipment.

Focus: The ability to bring your full and complete attention to a precise, central point.

The Four Critical Keys to Conquering Anything™: A simplified and prioritized process for strategic thinking and planning represented by the acronym ACTE.

Hardening the target: The deliberate attempt by a security force to stack every possible advantage in their favor in an effort to make their "protectee" or "principal" appear so difficult a challenge that the potential attacker moves on to another target.

Improved Outcome Formula™: A formula that demonstrates that when you work harder on controlling yourself than you do trying to control your situation, your outcomes improve.

Inflatable Boat Small (IBS): A small, six-man rubber boat used in BUD/S.

Intuition: The result of using one, if not all, of your five senses—hearing, seeing, feeling, smelling, tasting—to optimum effect, in combination with evaluated experience of past events.

Jacob's ladder: A large rope ladder with wooden steps specifically designed to board the uneven and slick sides of naval vessels.

JP5: A type of jet fuel.

The Mind Lab: A tool progressively developed with the student to enhance creative visual imagery for virtual training experiences.

Mission: A series of primary and secondary targets that, when knocked down, accomplish a major objective.

Movement: A series of actions or activities intended to arrive at a particular end. The process of using a weapon to knock down a target.

Naval Special Warfare (NSW): The command structure that oversees all special operations units in the navy.

Phase Diagram: A scheduling tool used in mission planning to clearly and independently see each phase of the mission and how it flows in relation to timed objectives.

Power: The ability to act.

Primaries: Clearly identified targets that are positioned right in front of you. They must be knocked down before you can take the next step on the path of accomplishing the overall goal or mission.

Rally point: A designated location to conduct rendezvous or linkups during field operations.

ROK marine: A Republic of Korea marine.

SEAL (SEa Air Land): Acronym for how this elite unit can insert, infiltrate, attack, exfiltrate, and extract from any environment, under any imaginable condition.

Secondaries: Tentative targets positioned behind your selected primary targets so that you are constantly moving forward toward the overall goal or mission.

Sniper bubble: The process a sniper uses to shut off the outside world in order to intensely focus on the task at hand.

Sniper cell: A self-contained designated unit of scout/snipers.

Stacked rubber duck: A platform with two rubber boats placed on top of each other to expedite airborne ocean insertions.

Standard Operating Procedures (SOP): A recognized then adopted pattern which assures a specific level of performance that produces faster results reliably. A fail-safe process to get things done.

Target: An object or goal to be reached.

The Three Core Questions of a Plan: How do I get there? What do I do when I get there? How do I get *out* of there?

The Three Dynamic Elements of Combat™: The understanding that targets dictate weapons, and weapons dictate movement. Without a clear target in mind, the process of choosing weapons and/or movement for their own sake is an exercise in futility.

Training Pyramid: A process of designing a training program to ensure new skills are thoroughly developed from a solid foundation to a level where an individual can perform accurately and knock down a target with appropriate speed.

Verbal Command Request™: A command you use on yourself or another that is structured in a specific way to elicit a known result.

Verbal-Influence Conditioning: The understanding that words influence our thoughts and condition our actions.

Vietcong: A Communist-led army and guerrilla force in South Vietnam that fought its government and was supported by North Vietnam.

Warrior: An individual who is so prepared to face the challenge before him and believes so strongly in the cause he is fighting for that he refuses to quit.

Weapon: Any skill, instrument, or device designed to knock down targets.

Zen: A discipline, study, or practice developed for the direct purpose of reaching enlightenment.

About the Author

Richard Machowicz founded the Bukido Institute in Marina del Rey, California. A ten-year veteran of the U.S. Navy SEALs, Machowicz participated in numerous tactical operations while attached to SEAL Team One and Two. While at SEAL Team Two he was assigned to the training cadre as the leading petty officer of Land, Mountain, and Arctic Warfare. He has more than seventeen years of experience in the martial arts, studying such systems as muay thai boxing, Jeet Kune Do, kickboxing, aikido, jujitsu, savate, arnis, and karate. He was a certified instructor in Naval Special Warfare Combat Fighting Instructor Course (the U.S. Navy SEAL hand-to-hand combat instructor course), and received multiple black belts. Machowicz has served as a personal protection specialist for high profile individuals within the political arena, business world, and entertainment industry. He is a member of the Screen Actors Guild and lives in southern California.

If you want more information about the Bukido Institute, its products, classes, and nationwide seminars, check out the web site at: www.bukido.com